Costumes

Those attending the party — volunteers, children and parents — should be encouraged to dress in costumes. Be sure to specify in ads and posters that the costumes should represent positive images, such as Bible characters, friendly animals or other non-ghoulish themes. However, if a child arrives in a "scary" costume, accept him or her gladly. An outreach event such as this should focus on acceptance so children will feel welcome to return for regular church classes and services.

List or illustrate several costume ideas in the advertisements and posters. More people will be willing to dress in costumes if you give them ideas for creating them easily and inexpensively. Patterns for costumes are on pages 85-105. Make them available in advance through the church office. These ideas provide children unrestricted vision and movement so they can easily play games. At longer parties, a booth could be included where children can make a simple costume. Safety is always a concern. Be sure to cover any staples used in costume construction with clear tape to prevent scratches. Fit costumes so children can move freely to play the games.

Theme Parties

You can use this book to create a variety of parties year-round. If your church is smaller or you are working with a limited budget, consider using selected parts of *The Un-Halloween Book* for your fall festival. Or, choose a theme for a party any time of the year. Either way, the following list will make planning easier.

Daniel and the Lions' Den
Game: Daniel and the Lions' Den, page 29
Craft: Pom-pom Lion Pencil Topper, page 55
Snack: Lion Crackers, page 80
Puzzle: What's Missing? page 70
Costume: Lion, page 93

Walls of Jericho
Game: Walls of Jericho, page 42
Snack: Building Blocks, page 74
Puzzle: Dot-to-Dot, page 61
Costume: Soldier, page 105

Noah and the Ark
Game: Noah and the Ark, page 37
Craft: Ark and Animals, page 47
Snack: Rainbow on a Cloud, page 81
Snack: Elephant Trunks, page 77
Snack: Zebra Brownies, page 84
Costume: Animals, pages 87-95

This Little Light of Mine

Game: This Little Light of Mine, page 41
Craft: Luminaries, page 54
Snack: Shining Candle, page 82
Costume: Candle, page 100

The Beatitudes

Game: Beatitudes Bee Hives, page 27
Craft: Buzzin' Bees, page 49
Puzzle: How Many Bees?, page 67
Costume: Bee, page 95
Costume: Flower, page 102

Fishing in the Sea of Galilee

Game: Fishing in the Sea of Galilee, page 31
Craft: Fishing Boat, page 50
Craft: Stuffed Fish, page 57
Snack: Special Catch, page 83
Costume: Fisherman, page 101

David and Goliath

Game: David and Goliath, page 30
Snack: Giant Pretzels, page 79
Activity: David and Goliath Coloring Page, page 63
Costume: Bible Characters, pages 96-97

The Parable of the Lost Sheep

Game: Lost Sheep, page 35
Snack: Animal Cut-Out Cookies, page 73
Puzzle: Find the Sheep's Twin, page 64

New Life

Game: New Life Cocoon, page 36
Craft: Butterfly Plant Stick, page 48
Snack: Butterfly Pizza, page 75
Costume: Butterfly, page 99

General Usage

Activities with this symbol can be
used with any theme.

Set-Up

Prior to the party, plan where each activity will be positioned. Determine which activities will need tables and how many. Give each activity as much space as possible.

The games can also be set up different classrooms or in a large open space, such as a fellowship hall. Define space in a large open area by placing tables in a U-shape. Each game can be labeled with large handmade or computer-generated banners. Include the suggested age range for the game.

Decorations

Use pumpkins, scarecrows, corn stalks and other items that suggest fall and harvest for this seasonal party. Good colors are orange, red, black, brown, yellow and green. Many of the games can have backdrops that would add to a festive look. Do not use images that promote Halloween, such as witches, devils, ghosts, black cats or tombstones.

The following decorations can be made two or three weeks in advance with the help of older children in Sunday school or youth group.

Painted Pumpkins

What You Need
❑ pumpkins
❑ pencils
❑ acrylic paint
❑ paintbrushes
❑ fabric paint

What to Do

1. Wash and dry a pumpkin.

2. Create your own design.

3. Use a pencil to draw features on the surface of the pumpkin. Remember, big designs are easier to paint.

4. Paint with acrylic paint. It may take more than one coat for complete coverage. Wait until the first coat dries before adding a second.

5. When the acrylic paint has dried, add a finished look by outlining the features with fabric paint. Add a white dot of shiny fabric paint to the pumpkin's black eyes.

Corn Stalks

What You Need
- ❏ brown or tan raffia
- ❏ toilet paper tubes
- ❏ brown poster paper
- ❏ broom handles
- ❏ buckets
- ❏ sand
- ❏ masking tape
- ❏ green crepe paper

What to Do
1. Place approximately one dozen 12-14" pieces of raffia in the middle of one empty toilet paper tube.
2. Wrap the tube and raffia in a 12"x12" piece of brown poster paper (or a paper grocery bag).
3. Twist the paper at the top of the tube with the raffia extending out the end.
4. Assemble a cornstalk on a broom handle that has been put into a bucket of sand.
5. Tape the bottom of the ear of corn to the broom handle using masking tape. Tape several ears to one pole. Be sure the ears of corn are angled up and are on all sides.
6. Wrap the entire handle with a roll of green crepe paper.

Indian Corn

What You Need
- ❏ toilet paper tubes
- ❏ scissors
- ❏ construction paper: yellow, tan, orange, gold, brown and maroon
- ❏ glue
- ❏ pattern on page 145

What to Do
1. Flatten one end of an empty toilet paper tube and make it narrower by trimming that end.
2. Cut corn husks from yellow or tan construction paper.
3. Glue the corn husks inside the uncut end of the tube.
4. Reproduce the kernel pattern on page 145 onto construction paper in shades of yellow, gold, orange, brown and maroon.
5. Cut out the individual kernels and glue them on the tube, covering the toilet paper tube with a variety of colors.

Paper Sack Pumpkins

What You Need
- ❑ brown paper sacks
- ❑ newspaper
- ❑ green yarn
- ❑ orange paint
- ❑ paintbrushes
- ❑ yellow felt
- ❑ scissors

What to Do
1. Half-fill brown paper sacks of various sizes with crumpled newspaper.
2. Squeeze and twist the top of the bag to make a stem. Tie closed with green yarn.
3. Paint the stuffed paper sack orange. Allow to dry.
4. Cut eyes, nose and mouth from yellow felt. Glue them onto the sack.

Scarecrow

What You Need
- ❑ jeans
- ❑ flannel shirts
- ❑ straw hats
- ❑ straw
- ❑ pumpkins
- ❑ paint
- ❑ paint brushes
- ❑ chairs

What to Do
1. Collect old jeans, flannel shirts and straw hats. Purchase straw and a pumpkin for each scarecrow.
2. Stuff the shirt and pants with straw.
3. Paint a face on a pumpkin for the scarecrow's head. Put a hat on the pumpkin. Prop the body in a chair and balance the pumpkin on top.

Note: Crumpled newspaper works well for stuffing if straw is limited or unavailable.

Fodder Shock

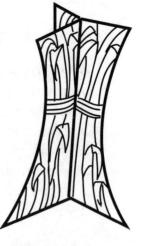

What You Need
- ❏ pattern from page 123
- ❏ yellow or tan construction paper
- ❏ scissors
- ❏ glue

What to Do
1. Reproduce onto yellow or tan paper the pattern of the group of corn stalks on page 123. You will need three for each fodder shock.
2. Cut out the three stalks then fold each in half lengthwise.

3. Glue the right half of each corn stalk to the left half of another (see right).
4. This 3-D fodder shock can stand on tables or be hung from the ceiling.

Spiraling Leaves

What You Need
- ❏ spiral pattern from page 147
- ❏ leaf patterns from page 149
- ❏ construction paper in fall colors
- ❏ heavy weight paper
- ❏ scissors
- ❏ glue, tape or stapler

What to Do
1. Reproduce the spiral pattern, on page 147, onto heavy weight paper, and the leaf patterns, on page 149, onto construction paper.
2. Cut along the line of the spiral.
3. Cut leaves from several different fall colors of construction paper.
4. Glue, tape or staple leaves along the spiral.
5. Hang the leaves from the ceiling.

Table Tents

What You Need
❏ pattern on page 119
❏ orange construction paper
❏ glue
❏ tape
❏ pencils or pens
❏ assorted fall decorations

What to Do
1. (These are for advertising your party.) Reproduce the pattern on page 119 on orange construction paper.
2. Cut out the pumpkin and fold it along the dotted lines.
3. Write the information on both sides of the pumpkin.
4. Glue the stems together.
5. Tape the folded rectangular section to the table.
6. Once placed, decorate around the tents with mini-pumpkins, gourds, leaves and acorns to make them more eye-catching.

Follow-Up and Evaluation

It is important that you keep in touch with the children and adults who attend the party, particularly those who are new to your church. The registration forms that people complete when they arrive at the party are a simple way to compile a list of contacts. Have your follow-up committee personally contact each child and adult visitor to invite them to worship at your church, either by phone or letter. A sample follow-up letter is on page 151. Evaluation questions are below. Only include the evaluation for adults. You might want to create evaluation questions for your volunteer staff as well. Be sure to enclosed a self-addressed, stamped envelope or print the questions on a stamped postcard for easy return.

Sample Evaluation Questions

Thank you for attending our Fall Festival Party. Please take a moment to complete the questions below and provide us with any comments you have regarding the party.

[Include ample space for writing responses.]

1. Were you satisfied with the quality of the games?

2. Was the cost appropriate?

3. Did your child enjoy the variety of prizes?

4. Did your child enjoy the crafts?

5. Was the biblical content appropriate for this type of party? Please explain.

6. Was the event held at a convenient time?

7. Would you return next year?

After the event is over, gather all of the materials and file them away for next year. Place all of the reproducible patterns from this book in their own files so you can easily access them again. Before the booths are dismantled, take a photograph of each to place on file. These will assist you in reconstructing the booths again next year.

Finally, write an evaluation of the event. Which activities worked well? Which didn't? What were some positive outcomes or comments (you can use these in next year's publicity!)? Were there any problems that could have been avoided? How would you like to conduct this event differently?

Then file it away, pour yourself a cup of apple cider, prop up your feet and thank God for all of the blessings your church has bestowed on His children.

Games

Beatitudes Bee Hives Ages 3-12

Bible Reference: The Beatitudes, Matthew 5:3-11

Overview

The "Bee-attitudes" sounds like a place where you would hear bees buzzing around. Have fun with this play on words as you introduce children to the ways Jesus taught us to live to be blessed. The children use a golf club to send bees into hives.

Helpers: 2
• 1 to accept and distribute tickets
• 1 to retrieve the balls

Materials
❑ eight 12-oz. frozen juice cans, empty and washed
❑ bee hive pattern on page 153
❑ yellow construction paper or card stock for bee hive
❑ yellow golf balls
❑ black permanent marker
❑ child-sized golf club
❑ masking tape or chalk

Preparation
1. Use the pattern on page 153 to make eight bee hives from construction paper or card stock.
2. Write one of the following phrases on each beehive:
   Blessed are the poor in spirit; Blessed are those who mourn; Blessed are the meek; Blessed are those who hunger and thirst for righteousness; Blessed are the merciful; Blessed are the pure in heart; Blessed are the peacemakers; Blessed are those who are persecuted because of righteousness.
3. Glue a beehive to the end of a juice can then cut out the opening.
4. Draw three lines with a permanent black marker around the golf ball to make it look like a bumblebee body. Note: If you cannot find yellow golf balls, spray paint white ones yellow.
5. Position the hives on the floor so that some are easier to hit than others. Note: If you are playing on a tile floor, you may need to tape the hives to the floor to keep them from moving when the ball goes into the juice can. Make a line on the floor with chalk indicating where the children will putt.

How to Play
1. Children putt the ball into the closest beehive.
2. The helper should read the beatitude on the beehive the golf ball hits or comes closest to. He or she should offer a brief explanation of what the words in the beatitude mean.
3. With each successful shot, children earn a chance to putt again, and a prize ticket.

Variation: You could have fewer than eight hives and make scenery, using the coloring page on page 223 as your pattern. Hang it behind the game with the rest of the Beatitudes printed on the background paper.

Belly of a Whale *Ages 6-12*

Bible Reference: Jonah and the Whale, Jonah 1-2

Overview
The children will crawl through a cardboard tunnel, simulating the whale. If the room has two doors, children can enter through one door and exit through the second. If not, arrange the maze in the room so that the children crawl through the tunnel, double back and exit through the same door.

Helpers: 2
• one person to accept tickets
• one person to squirt people

Materials
❑ one large room with two entrances, if possible
❑ appliance boxes
❑ whale pattern, on page 155
❑ carpet tubes (core in a roll of carpet)
❑ duct tape
❑ damp sponges
❑ ocean sounds (CD or cassette available at music stores)
❑ red light bulb
❑ extension cord
❑ spray mist bottle

Preparation
1. Cut cardboard to cover the entrance of the room. Enlarge the whale pattern on page 155 to fill the cardboard (see page 13 for how to enlarge patterns). Draw the whale on the cardboard and position it over the doorway.
2. Cut an opening at the mouth large enough for children to crawl through.
3. Place damp sponges near the entrance as the tongue.
4. Ribs can be made from large carpet tubes. Tape them together to make an arched structure.
5. Place long tables on their sides with a flattened appliance box as the roof. This makes a tunnel. Use duct tape to connect boxes.
6. Have a helper stationed somewhere in the room to squirt water on the children as they pass by.
7. Have the room very dark with a red light (pulsing on and off, if possible) near the middle.
8. Play a recording of crashing waves, seagulls and other ocean sounds.

How to Play
1. The ticket taker asks, **Do you know why Jonah was on a ship?** (He was running away from God.) **God wanted Jonah to tell the people of Nineveh that they needed to follow God. Jonah tried to run away from God but he ended up inside the belly of a fish!**
2. Then the ticket taker shouts, **Man overboard!** as each child enters the tunnel.
3. Limit the number of children inside the whale to two or three at a time. The children may crawl along slowly, using their hands to feel their way through the tunnel.
4. No prize ticket is given for this game.

Daniel and the Lions' Den *Ages 4-8*

Bible Reference: Daniel and the Lions' Den, Daniel 6

Overview

The children throw balls, trying to get them to stick to the whiskers of the lions.

Helpers: 2

• one person to accept and distribute tickets and hand out the balls
• one person to retrieve the balls

Materials

❑ lion pattern, on page 157
❑ white paper
❑ colored markers
❑ three ping-pong balls
❑ Velcro strips
❑ glue
❑ bulletin board
❑ thumb tacks
❑ masking tape or chalk
❑ tickets

Preparation

1. Use the lion pattern on page 157 and make several "whiskerless" lions.
2. Color the lions.
3. Cut them out and attach them to the wall.
4. Glue the loop side of the Velcro strips to the ping-pong balls.
5. Attach the fuzzy side of the Velcro strips as the whiskers for the lions.
6. Mark a line with masking tape or chalk about six feet from the lions as the place the children should stand.

How to Play

1. Children stand behind the line and throw the balls one at a time at the lions.
2. If any ball sticks, children are given two prize tickets. Everyone earns one ticket for trying.
3. The helper should ask the children, **Why are the lions' mouths closed?** (Because God protected Daniel when he was thrown in with the lions.)

David and Goliath *Ages 6-12*

Bible Reference: David and Goliath, 1 Samuel 17

Overview
Kids love the story of little David waging a battle against big Goliath. In this game, the children throw bean bags at Goliath, simulating David slinging the stone at him.

Helpers: 2
- one to accept and distribute tickets
- one to retrieve the beanbags

Materials
- ❑ large piece of plywood
- ❑ white poster paper
- ❑ Goliath pattern, page 159
- ❑ markers or crayons
- ❑ stapler
- ❑ felt
- ❑ dried beans
- ❑ needle
- ❑ thread

Preparation
1. Cut several holes on a large piece of plywood.
2. Make a support for the target to stand.
3. Cover the target with white poster paper.
4. Enlarge the picture of Goliath, on page 159. (See page 13 for how to enlarge patterns.)
5. Paint or color the picture of Goliath.
6. Cut holes in the picture to match the holes of the target.
7. Make five beanbags from two 5" square pieces of felt each. Sew around three edges.
8. Fill the pouch with dried beans and sew the fourth side shut.

How to Play
1. The helper gives the player five beanbags.
2. The player tries to hit the holes in the target. If children succeed with four or five beanbags, they receive three prize tickets. If they succeed with two or three beanbags, they receive two tickets. Everyone gets one ticket for trying.
3. As the helper hands the child the beanbag, he or she should say, **Do you know how many tries it took for David to hit Goliath? Just one try, because God helped him.**

Fishing in the Sea of Galilee *Ages 3-8*

Bible Reference: The Miraculous Catch, John 21:3-6

Overview

The children "go fishing" by throwing a net over a backdrop.

Helpers: 3

- one person to take tickets
- two people to tape tickets to the fish's mouth and tug on the net

Materials

- ❑ cardboard appliance box
- ❑ scissors
- ❑ paint
- ❑ paint brush
- ❑ fish net
- ❑ grocery bag fish (see craft on page 57)
- ❑ tape

Preparation

1. Cut a piece of cardboard from the appliance box that is large enough to cover a door opening.

2. Paint an ocean scene on one side (see illustration at left).

3. Tape the backdrop in front of an open door. Leave a two- to three-foot opening at the top for the net to be tossed over. (Helpers will be seated inside the room and ready the fish for catching.)

4. See page 57 for how to make the grocery bag fish. Have a stockpile of fish, several of which have a prize ticket taped to their mouths.

How to Play

1. Children throw one end of the net over the backdrop.

2. When they feel a tug on the net, they bring the net back to their side of the door. The first time the net should be empty. A worker should say, **The disciples went fishing once and didn't catch anything. Jesus told them to throw the net again. Try again and see what happens this time.**

3. The child throws the net over the backdrop again and this time several fish should be in the net. The child should look at each fish until he or she finds the one with the prize ticket attached. The helper should remove the ticket and give it to the child, then toss the fish back.

Fruits of the Spirit *Ages 8-12*

Bible Reference: The Fruit of the Spirit, Galatians 5:22-23

Overview

Like fruit on a tree, these balloons that children attempt to burst are filled with something sweet — the fruit of the Spirit. If they did not know about the fruit of the Spirit before, they will learn some of those attributes with this game.

Helpers: 2
- one person to accept tickets and distribute darts
- one person to replace the balloons on the board

Materials
❑ poster paper
❑ large bulletin board
❑ thumb tacks
❑ balloons
❑ darts
❑ list of Fruits of the Spirit, page 163
❑ tree pattern, page 161
❑ markers or crayons
❑ tape
❑ chalk or masking tape
❑ Bible

Preparation
1. Enlarge the tree pattern on page 161 on poster paper and color it in. (See page 13 for how to enlarge patterns.)
2. Fasten the poster paper to a large bulletin board.
3. Reproduce the characteristics on page 163. Cut the words apart, roll them up and put one inside each balloon before they are inflated.
4. Inflate the balloons and tie a knot in each end. Tape the knotted end of the balloons to the tree to resemble fruit. Have additional balloons ready to refill the tree as they are popped.
5. Make a line on the floor with chalk or masking tape for the children to stand to toss the darts. You may want to have two lines for older and younger children.

How to Play
1. Take extreme caution with the darts. Have spectators stand far back from the dart-throwing.
2. Children stand on the line and throw three darts. If they pop a balloon, they earn one prize ticket. They earn a second ticket by reading the paper inside the balloon and answering the question from the helper, **Is that one of the fruits of the Spirit?** If they do not know the answer let them look up Galatians 5:22 and read the passage. (Read the verse out loud to non-readers.)
3. If children do not pop a balloon, let them earn a ticket by answering the question, **Is that one of the fruits of the Spirit?** using a strip of paper from a previously popped balloon.

God Provides Manna *Ages 3-8*

Bible Reference: God Sends Manna to His children, Exodus 16

Overview

God provided abundant food for the Israelites. In this game, children collect "manna" in their baskets during a set time period. This is not a contest to see who can collect the most.

Helpers: 2

- one person to accept and distribute tickets
- one person to weigh baskets and return manna to wading pool

Materials

- ❏ foam packing pieces, approximately a trash bag full
- ❏ wading pool
- ❏ four small baskets
- ❏ stop watch
- ❏ scale

Preparation

Put the foam packing pieces into an empty wading pool. Do not put water in the pool!

How to Play

1. Allow three or four children to stand in the wading pool at a time.
2. At the leader's signal, the children try to put as much manna as they can in their baskets in 15 seconds.
3. At the end of the time period, weigh each basket and pronounce it "Just the right amount."
4. Award each child a prize ticket.
5. A helper should say, **God provided the manna to the Israelites while they were in the desert. Each day the Israelites were to gather just enough food for their family for the day. God still provides for our needs today.**

Good Samaritan _Ages 4-10_

Bible Reference: The Good Samaritan, Luke 10:25-37

Overview

This game is a variation of "Pin the Tail on the Donkey." Instead of pinning a tail, the children will attach a bandage to the hurt man.

Helpers: 3

- one person to accept tickets, put the blindfold on players and spin them
- one person to distribute bandages and prize tickets
- one person to open bandages

Materials

❑ poster paper
❑ injured person pattern, page 165
❑ clear, self-stick plastic
❑ markers
❑ masking tape
❑ blindfold
❑ adhesive bandages
❑ wastebasket
❑ tickets

Preparation

1. On a piece of poster paper, enlarge the pattern of the injured person on page 165. (See page 13 for how to enlarge a pattern.)
2. Make several marks on the arms, legs, face, etc., to represent cuts.
3. Cover the picture with clear, self-stick plastic or laminate it so that the applied bandages can be easily removed.
4. Hang the picture on the wall.

How to Play

1. Hand the child an unwrapped adhesive strip with the instruction to try to place it on one of the man's wounds in the drawing after he or she is blindfolded.
2. The worker should say, **There was a man in Bible times who was robbed and beaten and left along the road to die. Some of the people who passed by would not help him, but one person did. Let's pretend that you are that one person called the Good Samaritan. Try to put this bandage on one of the man's wounds.**
3. The child playing the game is blindfolded and spun around.
4. Point the child in the direction of the wall where the picture is hanging.
5. The child should try to place the adhesive bandage on one of the wounds. If the child succeeds, he or she is awarded two prize tickets. Participants receive one.

Lost Sheep *Ages 3-12*

Bible Reference: The Parable of the Lost Sheep, Luke 15:4-6

Overview

Just like Jesus takes care of His lost children, this game challenges children to use a shepherd's staff to capture the lost sheep.

Helpers: 2

- 1 takes tickets and gives tickets
- 1 resets the sheep for the next player

Materials

- ❏ sheep from page 167
- ❏ two toilet paper tubes per sheep
- ❏ two craft sticks per sheep
- ❏ 20" of 14-gauge wire, one per sheep
- ❏ 10" of foam, square or round, one per sheep
- ❏ 3' walking cane or foam cane
- ❏ masking tape or chalk
- ❏ page 217, optional

Preparation

1. Punch a hole on one side of each toilet paper tube near the top.
2. Hook one end of the wire through the hole and twist to secure it. Do the same with the other end of the wire and the other tube.
3. Cut out two sheep.
4. Glue a sheep on either side of the tubes. The wire between the two tubes will make a large loop for the children to hook when they are finding their lost sheep.
5. Position the sheep on the foam and mark where the feet are. Insert one craft stick into the foam where each leg will be.

6. Put the toilet paper tubes over the craft sticks so the sheep will stand during the game.
7. Make as many sheep as your space will allow so that the game will be challenging.
8. This game can be played on a tabletop or on the floor. Position the sheep so that some are easy to reach. If playing on the floor, mark an area that the children must stand behind.
9. Use page 217 to make a background with lots of sheep.

How to Play

1. The child playing uses the cane to try to pick up the "lost" sheep from its craft stick stand.
2. Tell the child that he or she is helping the shepherd to round up his lost sheep. Give the child several opportunities to ring the lost sheep.
3. Say to the children, **Jesus cares about each and every person, just as a shepherd looks after all his sheep.**
4. Every successful ring wins a prize ticket.
5. Return the sheep to the stands for the next child to play.

New Life Cocoon *Ages 3-12*

Bible Reference: Jesus' Resurrection and New Life, Romans 6:4

Overview

The butterfly emerging from a cocoon is an analogy often used to describe Jesus' resurrection. In this game, children will try to drop a caterpillar into a cocoon.

Helpers: 1

- one person to accept and distribute tickets and give caterpillars

Materials

- ❏ coffee can
- ❏ clear tape
- ❏ brown paper
- ❏ clothespins, any type
- ❏ brown chenille stems
- ❏ tickets

Preparation

1. Cover a large coffee can with brown paper.
2. Make several caterpillars by wrapping a clothespin with brown chenille stems.
3. Use some of the Butterfly Plant Sticks on page 48 to decorate the area.

How to Play

1. Place coffee can "cocoon" on the floor.
2. Give each child three caterpillars. Children stand over the can and try to drop a clothespin "caterpillar" into the can.
3. Award a prize ticket for two or three successful attempts.
4. Ask the children, **Do you know what the caterpillar emerges as from the cocoon?** (butterfly) Continue with something like, **That reminds me of how Jesus was placed in the tomb on Good Friday and came out alive on Sunday. Because of Jesus, we, too, can have new life.**

Noah and the Ark Ages 3-8

Bible Reference: Noah and the Ark, Genesis 6–8

Overview

Noah took a pair of every animal on the ark to preserve them from the flood. In this game, the children toss pairs of plastic animals onto a floating boat.

Helpers: 2

- one person to accept and distribute tickets
- one person to get the animals out of the water

Materials

- ❑ baby bathtub or water table
- ❑ foam meat trays
- ❑ pint milk carton
- ❑ scissors
- ❑ brown construction paper
- ❑ hot glue gun
- ❑ glue
- ❑ small plastic animals (four pairs)
- ❑ towel
- ❑ chalk or masking tape

Preparation

1. Turn a large foam meat tray into a boat by trimming it as shown at right.
2. Cut the top off of the milk carton, leaving an open box into which children will toss the animals.
3. Cover the sides of the milk carton with brown construction paper and glue it to the meat tray to be the ark structure. Be sure the glue isn't so hot that it melts the tray.
4. Make a line on the floor with chalk or masking tape.
5. Put water in the tub or table.

How to Play

1. Children are to stand at the line and toss the plastic animals one at a time into the ark.
2. If children get any pair of animals into the ark they win two prize tickets.
3. Everyone earns one ticket for trying.
4. Ask the players, **Do you know how many of each kind of animal Noah took on the ark?** (two each) **Do you know who went on the ark with Noah?** (Noah's wife and Noah's sons and their wives.)

Puzzle Piece Search Ages 3-12

Bible Reference: general Bible knowledge

Overview
To help children understand that they can look to the Bible for the answers to life's puzzles, have them look for the hidden puzzle pieces and find their matches.

Helpers: 1
• one to signal the start of the game, verify correct matches and award tickets

Materials
❑ puzzle piece pattern, on page 169
❑ medium-weight paper
❑ copy machine or pencil to trace pattern
❑ scissors
❑ table

Preparation
1. Reproduce the puzzle piece pattern on page 169 onto medium-weight paper.
2. Cut the pattern into two pieces.
3. On each piece, write one word from a pair of words that go together. Examples: David and Goliath, Fishing and Sea of Galilee, Widow and Lost Coin, Good Shepherd and Lost Sheep, Jesus and New Life, Moses and the Hebrew People, Pharaoh and the Plagues, Daniel and the Lions' Den, Jonah and the Whale, Joshua and Jericho. Make several sets.
4. For younger children, or an easier game, make each cut distinct. The game will be more difficult if all of the pattern pieces have the same cut.
5. This game is best played in a classroom where the door can be closed while hiding the puzzle pieces.
6. Set a table in the center of the room.
7. Place one piece of each two-piece puzzle on the table.
8. Hide the remaining pieces around the room.

How to Play
1. Children gather outside the room for this game. At the helper's signal, a few children enter the room and each searches for one hidden puzzle piece.
2. When a child finds one (and only one), he or she takes it to the table and finds the matching piece.
3. The child gives the match to the leader and receives a prize ticket.
4. If desired, a helper can have the children tell why the words on the two puzzle pieces go together before awarding the ticket. If you add this feature to the game, you may wish to have more than one helper, depending on how many children come into the room at one time.
5. Before the children leave, the helper should say, **The answers to all the puzzles in life are found in the Bible.**

Search for the Lost Coin *Ages 3-8*

Bible Reference: The Parable of the Lost Coin, Luke 15:8-10

Overview

Even children know the frustration over losing something important. This game demonstrates how much we value finding something, just like Jesus values finding us as His children.

Helpers: 2

- one person to accept and distribute tickets
- one person to bury the coins

Materials

❑ baby bathtub
❑ sand
❑ ten pennies
❑ stop watch

Preparation

1. Pour sand into the baby bathtub or similarly-sized tub.
2. Bury one penny in the sand.
3. Place the other nine coins in view.

How to Play

1. Each child has 15 seconds to find the lost coin.
2. The children may exchange the penny for a prize ticket.
3. The helper should say, **Have you ever lost something that is very important to you? Each and every one of us is very important to Jesus. He loves us very much.**

Ten Plagues *Ages 3-8*

Bible Reference: God's Plagues on Pharoah, Exodus 7:14-11:10

Overview

Children playing this game will learn about the plagues God brought on Pharoah for his unholy behavior.

Helpers: 2

- one person takes tickets, names the plagues and gives tickets
- one person collects bean bags

Materials

❏ five shoe boxes
❏ patterns of plagues, pages 171-179
❏ glue
❏ old socks
❏ string
❏ rice
❏ chalk or masking tape
❏ crayons or markers

Preparation

1. Using the patterns on pages 171-179, reproduce the pictures of the ten plagues.
2. Color the pictures, then glue two inside each box.
3. Beanbags are simply made by pouring a cup of rice into a small sock and tying the end with a piece of string.
4. Mark a line on the floor with chalk or masking tape.
5. Space the five boxes at varied distances beyond the line.

How to Play

1. Children stand at the line and throw the beanbags one at a time at each box.
2. Children who get one beanbag in each of the five boxes earn three prize tickets. Give two tickets to children who get one to four beanbags in the boxes, and one ticket for trying.
3. A helper names each plague as the beanbag lands in a box.
4. At the end of the child's turn a helper should ask, **Do you know what Pharaoh said after the tenth plague? Leave my people, you and the Israelites! Go, worship the Lord.** (Exodus 12:31)

This Little Light of Mine *Ages 6-12*

Bible Reference: God Is Light, 1 John 1:5

Overview

Children will learn — as they spray water to extinguish candles — about getting rid of negative traits and who can help them do so.

Helpers: 3

- one person to accept and distribute tickets
- one person to light the candle
- one person to mop the floor

Materials

❑ six candles in secure holders
❑ 4" x 6" index cards
❑ markers
❑ clear, self-stick plastic
❑ long table
❑ matches
❑ two squirt guns or misting bottles
❑ masking tape or chalk
❑ stop watch

Preparation

1. Use masking tape or chalk to make a line on the floor where the children are to stand.
2. Make labels to set in front of the candles by folding the index cards in half. Write one of the following words on each card: Mine, Hate, Fear, Temptation, Worry and Sin.
3. Cover the cards with clear, self-stick plastic to keep them from getting wet.

How to Play

NOTE: Use extreme caution when playing this game. Be sure candles are not positioned near anything flammable. Be very strict about crowd control for this game, keeping children away from the candles.

1. Each child is given 20 seconds to use the squirt gun to blow out all of the candles except the one labeled "Mine."
2. One helper should read the label of each candle as it is extinguished.
3. Older children earn two prize tickets if the only candle left burning is the one labeled "Mine." Younger children can be given two tickets if they extinguish just one candle.
4. Everyone gets one ticket for playing.
5. Ask each of the children if they know how to extinguish those negative traits in their own lives. Ask, **What can you do if you start worrying?** or **Who can you ask to take away feelings of hatred?** (pray; ask Jesus)

Walls of Jericho *Ages 4-8*

Bible Reference: Joshua and the Fall of Jericho, Joshua 6

Overview

Just like the wall of Jericho fell, children will roll a ball and try to knock down a cardboard block wall.

Helpers: 2

- one person takes tickets, blows horn and gives tickets
- one person sets up the wall

Materials

❑ Jericho puzzle on page 211, optional
❑ large ball
❑ ten cardboard blocks, any size
❑ chalk or masking tape
❑ horn
❑ construction paper, self-stick paper or spray paint

Preparation

1. As an option, use the dot-to-dot of the city of Jericho, on page 211, as a pattern for a backdrop for this game. Connect the dots before enlarging the pattern!
2. Mark a line on the floor with the chalk or masking tape where children are to stand.
3. Rectangular blocks can be made out of clean half-gallon cardboard milk cartons. Cut the top off each carton. Force the open end of one carton over the open end of the second carton. Cover with construction paper, self-stick paper or spray paint.
4. Stack the blocks as shown.

How to Play

1. Before each child takes a turn, a helper should walk back and forth in front of the wall seven times. (A player can do this if they have seen it done while waiting for a turn. Do not let this step slow the game down.)
2. On the seventh pass he or she blows a horn, the signal to the player to roll the ball and try to knock down the block wall (see Joshua 6:15-16).
3. If the children knock down the entire wall they are given two prize tickets. Each child who tries gets one ticket.
4. The helper should say, **Joshua was a great leader of the Israelites. With God's help, the walls of the city of Jericho fell down.**

Water from the Rock *Ages 3-12*

Bible Reference: Moses Brings Water from a Rock, Exodus 17:1-7

Overview

No one expected water to come from a rock when Moses hit it. The children playing this game will earn a different kind of liquid reward when they hit the "rock."

Helpers: 2

- one person to accept tickets and position children
- one person to operate music and give winners soda

Materials

- ❏ lively recorded music
- ❏ clean trash can, 30 gallon size
- ❏ poster paper
- ❏ sponges
- ❏ gray paint
- ❏ construction paper
- ❏ stone pattern, on page 181
- ❏ clear tape
- ❏ 15" stick or wooden dowel
- ❏ several cans of soda

Preparation

1. Turn the trash can into a rock by taping poster paper to it. Cover the lid separately.
2. Sponge-paint the paper with gray paint and allow it to dry.
3. Place the cans of soda inside the trash can and attach the lid.
4. Put the stick on the floor nearby.
5. Make a path using construction paper cut using the stone pattern on page 181.
6. Place the stones in a kidney-shaped circle around the room. Be sure they are close enough together for children to step on them easily.
7. One stone should be close enough to the trash can to indicate a clear winner.

How to Play

1. Several children can play this game at once. Begin with each child standing on a stone.
2. While children are gathering, the helper should say, **God provided for the Israelites when they were wandering in the desert by allowing Moses to bring water from a rock. God still provides for us today.**
3. As the music plays, children walk from stone to stone. Vary the length of the time the music is played from 15 to 60 seconds.
4. When the music stops, the child closest to the rock strikes it with the stick.
5. The leader takes a can of soda from the trash can for that child.
6. The soda is the prize for this game. No tickets are given.

Wheel of Knowledge Ages 3-12

Bible Reference: general Bible knowledge

Overview

This game offers children a chance to demonstrate their Bible knowledge. Prompt those who may be new to Bible stories.

Helpers: 1

• one to help read the questions, judge the answers and award tickets

Materials

❏ arrow pattern, page 183
❏ poster board
❏ marker
❏ razor blade or craft knife
❏ paper fastener
❏ large paper clip

A.

B.

Fold

Cut

C.

D.

Preparation

1. Cut out a paper arrow and glue it to one side of a large paper clip (see Illustration A).
2. Cut two 15" circles from poster board.
3. Draw lines to divide one of the circles into six pie-shaped sections of equal size (see Illustration B).
4. Cut a flap in each pie-shape (see Illustration C).
5. Poke a hole in the middle of each circle.
6. Attach the two poster board circles together, with the large paper clip and arrow between the top circle and the paper fastener. The circle with the flaps should be on top (see Illustration D).
7. Write one Bible question (on page 183) on the bottom circle under each flap.

How to Play

1. Children play this game one at a time.
2. The child spins the paper clip and answers the question under the flap to which the arrow is pointing.
3. Correct answers are awarded a prize ticket.
4. Make more than one "Wheel of Knowledge" with questions of various levels of difficulty.
5. Have children use the wheel that is most appropriate for their age.
6. After the child has played the game ask, **Do you know where all the answers can be found? The Bible!**

Crafts

Ark and Animals *Ages 3-8*

Bible Reference: Noah and the Ark, Genesis 7:1-3

Overview
Children cut and color a paper ark and animals.

Helpers: 1
• one for every 5-6 children

Materials
❑ ark and animal patterns, on pages 185-191
❑ medium-weight paper
❑ scissors
❑ clear tape
❑ crayons or markers

Preparation
1. Reproduce the patterns on medium weight paper.
2. Cut out the animals and ark for very young children.

Note: The ark pattern can be enlarged and used as a backdrop for the Noah and the Ark game on page 37.

What to Do
1. The children should color and cut out the ark and animals.
2. Show how to fold the animals on either side of the base so they stand on the flat base. Place a piece of tape at the top of each animal to secure it.
3. Suggest that the children write their names or initials inside the figures. They may use the figures to act out the events in the Bible story.
4. Ask, **The animals boarded the ark two-by-two. Which animals will you put on your ark first?**

Butterfly Plant Stick *Ages 3-12*

Bible Reference: Jesus' Resurrection and New Life, Romans 6:4

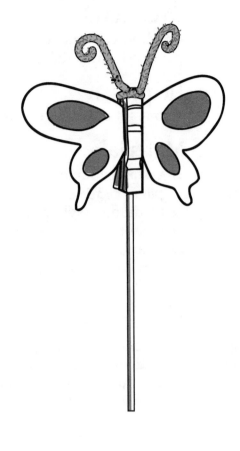

Overview

The children will assemble a construction paper butterfly and attach it to a stick.

Helpers: 1

• one for every 3-4 children

Materials

❑ spring-type clothespins
❑ colored paper
❑ colored tissue paper
❑ poster board
❑ butterfly pattern, on page 193
❑ butterfly insert pattern, on page 195
❑ pencils
❑ scissors
❑ white glue
❑ chenille wire
❑ 10" bamboo skewers or thin dowel rods
❑ hot glue gun, optional

Preparation

1. Duplicate the butterfly pattern on colored paper.
2. Trace the butterfly insert pattern on poster board to make templates for the children.
3. Pre-cut the patterns for very young children.

What to Do

1. Have the children cut two butterfly shapes from colored paper for each plant stick.
2. Show how to cut the openings in the butterfly wings where they are marked.
3. Have the children use a template to trace and cut out two inserts from tissue paper.
4. Show how to position the tissue paper on top of one opening cut in the butterfly wing so that the tissue covers it. Glue in place. Do the same with the other openings.
5. Demonstrate how to glue the two wings together, tissue sides facing in.
6. Help the children pull apart the two wooden pieces from the clothespin. This will form the body of the butterfly.
7. Show how to glue the assembled butterfly wings between the clothespin halves.
8. Explain how to twist a pipe cleaner around the top of the clothespin (butterfly body) to form antennae.
9. Show where to glue the butterfly on a skewer or thin dowel rod. You may want to use a hot glue gun on this final step to complete the project quickly. Hot glue dries in seconds and children can take the plant stick with them. But be sure an adult uses the glue gun.
10. Say, **The butterfly symbolizes new life — the new life we have in Jesus Christ.**

Buzzin' Bees *Ages 6-12*

Bible Reference: The Beatitudes, Matthew 5:3-11

Overview

The children will make a bumble bee hovering over a flower.

Helpers: 1

• one for every 4 children

Materials

❑ one 1$\frac{1}{2}$" foam ball per child
❑ yellow craft paint
❑ black chenille wire, one per child
❑ 10" white chenille wire, one per child
❑ black markers
❑ flower pattern, on page 197
❑ 10" wooden skewer, one per child
❑ one gallon milk jug cap, one per child
❑ drill

Preparation

1. Paint the foam ball yellow with yellow craft paint.
2. When it has dried, use a black marker to color stripes on the yellow ball to make the bee body.
3. Reproduce the flower pattern for each child.
4. Drill a hole in the milk jug caps that are the size of the skewer.
5. Cut the black chenille wire into three 2$\frac{1}{2}$" pieces for each child plus a tiny piece for a tail.

What to Do

1. Show how to make a loop from one 2$\frac{1}{2}$" piece of chenille wire and insert it on the side of the body to make a wing. Repeat for second wing.
2. To make antennae, show how to fold the third piece of the pipe cleaner in half and curl each end.
3. Have the children insert the folded end of the antennae into the ball.
4. Instruct them to add a short piece in back for the stinger.
5. Show where to insert the white pipe cleaner into the foam ball just below the stinger.
6. Allow the children to cut out and color the flower.
7. Show how to glue the completed flower to the top of the milk cap.
8. Help the children insert the skewer through the hole, punching a hole in the flower. Insert chenille wire attached to the bee through the top of the flower, and extend under cap.
9. Demonstrate how to wrap the free end of the white chenille wire around the skewer.
10. When the children spin the skewer, the bee will hover over the flower.
11. Say, **These bees remind me of the beatitudes. Jesus listed the beatitudes when He was teaching. The beatitudes list qualities toward which the Christian should strive.**

Fishing Boat Ages 3-6

Bible Reference: The Miraculous Catch, John 21:3-6

Overview

The children will create a soap boat.

Helpers: 1

• one for every 5 children

Materials

❑ Ivory soap flakes
❑ water
❑ mixing containers
❑ large spoons
❑ permanent marker
❑ 9" paper plates

What to Do

1. Pour the soap flakes into a container and add just enough water until the mixture is the consistency of play dough.

2. Give each child a piece of dough about the size of a tennis ball. Encourage the children to shape their ball into a fishing boat.

3. The boats need to harden over night, so it is better to send them home on a paper plate. They can be used as soap in the bathtub.

4. Say, **At least four of the disciples were fishermen. Do you think their boats looked like these? Jesus chose average, working people to be His followers. Jesus can use each one of us if we let Him.**

Note: A 32-ounce box of soap flakes will make approximately seven boats.

Good Shepherd Picture Frame *Ages 6-12*

Bible Reference: The Good Shepherd, John 10:14-16

Overview
The children will make a picture frame to remind them of Jesus.

Helpers: 1
• one for every 4-5 children

Materials
❏ eight craft sticks per child
❏ four craft foam sheep per child
❏ black paint
❏ paint brush
❏ glue
❏ scissors
❏ crayons or markers
❏ small sheets of paper
❏ picture of Jesus and Good Shepherd box, on page 199

Preparation
1. Make four craft foam sheep per frame using the pattern on page 199 for each child.
2. Paint the ears and muzzle black.
3. Duplicate the picture of Jesus and "Jesus is My Good Shepherd" for each child.

What to Do
1. Have the children position two craft sticks side by side to make the top of the frame.
2. Show how to position two craft sticks side by side to make the bottom of the frame.
3. Show how to position two craft sticks side by side, perpendicular to the top and bottom sticks. Have the children glue these in place, making the left side of frame.
4. Have them repeat step 3 to make the right side of frame (see illustration above).
5. Demonstrate how to trim the picture of Jesus to fill the opening and glue to the back of the frame. The children should color the picture of Jesus.
6. Show where to glue the paper with "Jesus is My Good Shepherd" on front at either the top or bottom or have the children write it on.
7. Allow the children to glue one sheep to each corner of the frame.
8. Say, **Calling Jesus our Good Shepherd means we know He will care for us.**

Variations
Instead of cutting sheep from foam, use stickers, cut sheep from paper or have children color the frame.

Instead of a picture of Jesus, take a Polaroid picture of the child to use for the picture.

Jonah Pop-Up *Ages 5-10*

Bible Reference: Jonah and the Whale, Jonah 1:15-17

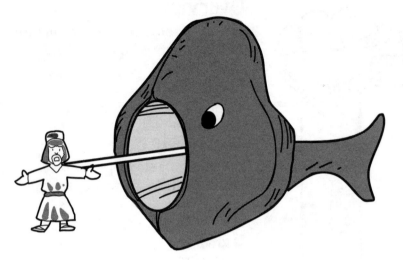

Overview

The children will turn a paper cup into a whale.

Helpers: 1

• one for every 4-5 children

Materials

❑ 5-oz. drinking cups
❑ plastic drinking straws
❑ whale head and tail pattern, on page 201
❑ Jonah pattern, on page 201
❑ pencils
❑ construction paper
❑ scissors
❑ glue
❑ tape

Preparation

1. Using a pencil, punch a hole in the end of each cup big enough for the straw.
2. Reproduce the patterns on pages 201 for each child.

What to Do

1. Have the children cut out two whales, two tails and one Jonah.
2. Show how to position the cup between the two whale head pieces and glue them on.
3. Show where to tape the paper whale head together at the top and bottom, encasing the cup (see illustration at right).
4. Leave the mouth end open.
5. Demonstrate how to slide the straw through the hole in the cup (see illustration at right).
6. Show how to tape Jonah to the end of the straw, coming out of the mouth.
7. Have the children glue the fin end of the tailpieces together around the other end of the straw.
8. Show where to tape the straight end of the tail to the straw. (The glue will not stick to the plastic.)
9. Say, **Jonah was swallowed by a big fish. That kept him from drowning in a storm at sea. When Jonah got out of the fish he did God's work, telling people the way they should live their lives.**

Leaf Mobile *Ages 5-12*

Seasonal

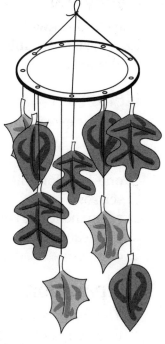

Overview
The children will make a mobile.

Helpers: 1
• one for every 5 children

Materials
❑ waxed paper
❑ crayon shavings in fall colors
❑ newspaper
❑ old towels
❑ iron
❑ leaf patterns, on page 203
❑ poster board
❑ plastic lids from coffee cans
❑ fishing line
❑ clear tape
❑ ironing board
❑ hole punch

Preparation
1. Use the leaf patterns on page 203 to make templates from poster board.
2. Punch nine evenly spaced small holes around the plastic lid (see illustration).
3. Cut fishing line into one 12" length and three 20" lengths per child.

What to Do
1. Cover the ironing surface with several layers of newspaper.
2. Use pieces of waxed paper that are no bigger than the ironing surface.
3. Allow the children to sprinkle crayon shavings around the surface of one piece of waxed paper.
4. Cover the shavings with another piece of waxed paper and place towel over the entire surface.
5. The helper should gently iron the towel at medium temperature. Be sure to exercise caution and keep children away from the warm iron.
6. Once all of the shavings are melted, set the waxed paper with melted shavings aside to cool.
7. Show how to use the leaf pattern template from page 203 to trace and cut out the leaf shapes from the waxed paper pieces. Each child will need six leaves.
8. Give each child a 12" length of fishing line and show how to thread it through every third hole.
9. Demonstrate how to gather the three pieces of line and tie them together to make a hanger for the mobile on the top side of the lid (see illustration).
   The remaining six holes are for the leaves.
10. Give each child three 20" lengths of fishing line and show how to thread one piece up through the bottom of one hole and back down through the top of the next hole. Repeat for the remaining two holes with other pieces of fishing line.
11. Help the children attach the leaves to the end of each line with tape. The project is ready to hang.
12. Quote Ecclesiastes 3:1 for the children. Say, **There is a time for everything, and a season for every activity under heaven.** Talk about fall and what changes this season brings. Ask, **What activities do you do in the fall?**

Luminaries *Ages 3-12*

Bible Reference: Let Your Light Shine, Matthew 5:16

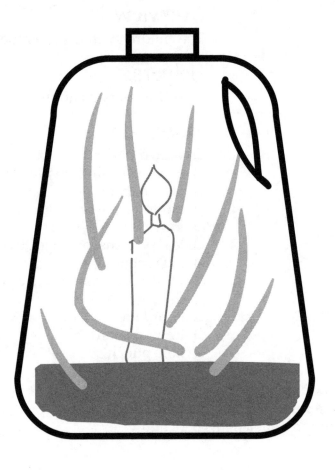

Overview
The children will make a luminaries to line the walkways.

Helpers: 1
• one for every four children

Materials
❑ one 1-gallon milk jug per child
❑ scissors
❑ permanent markers and stickers
❑ play sand
❑ one votive candle per child

Preparation
1. You will need one milk jug, three cups of sand and one votive candle per child.
2. Wash and dry the milk jugs.
3. Cut a three-sided door so that you reach inside the milk carton but can still shut the flap (see illustration).

What to Do
1. Give a pre-cut milk jug and permanent markers and stickers to the children to decorate their luminaries.
2. When they are finished decorating, add the sand to the jug and set a votive candle in it.
3. Position the jugs along the walkway and then ask an adult to light the candles. Caution the children that only adults are to light the candles.
4. Luminaries are a great way to let our lights shine for Jesus. Ask, **Have you ever been in the dark and someone turns on a flashlight or lights a candle? Doesn't everyone look to the light? To be a light for Jesus means everyone looks at what you do and sees it as a good example. When you live your life in a way that is pleasing to God you are letting your light shine.**

Pom-pom Lion Pencil Topper *Ages 6-12*

Bible Reference: Daniel and the Lions' Den, Daniel 6:16-22

Overview

The children will glue felt pieces to a pom-pom, making a lion to add to the end of a pencil.

Helpers: 1

• one for every three to four children

Materials

❑ unsharpened pencils
❑ thick craft glue
❑ scissors
❑ 1" gold or tan pom-poms
❑ 1/4" gold or tan pom-poms
❑ ears and nose patterns, page 205
❑ mane pattern, page 205
❑ felt, black and brown
❑ 2-3 mm plastic eyes
❑ black embroidery floss
❑ scissors

Preparation

1. You will need one 1" and two 1/4" pom-poms per child.
2. Cut a pair of ears from brown felt, a black felt nose and a brown felt mane for each child using the patterns. Cut a small "x" in the center of the mane circle.

What to Do

1. Show how to force a 1" pom-pom into the center opening of the mane. Glue if necessary.
2. Help the students fringe the circle of felt surround the lion's face.
3. Show where to glue on ears and eyes.
4. Have the students add one 1/4" pom-pom on either side of the nose.
5. Show how to glue two short pieces of embroidery floss straight down from the nose location and curve each outward for the mouth. The children should glue the nose on top of the floss (see illustration above).
6. The lion may then be glued onto the top of the pencil near the eraser.
7. Say, **Daniel was thrown into the lion's den because he disobeyed the king's law. But God kept Daniel safe because he obeyed God's law. The lions did not open their mouths.**

Pumpkin Pin *Ages 5-12*

Seasonal

Overview

The children make a pumpkin pin.

Helpers: 1

• one for every 5 children

Materials

❑ orange craft foam
❑ pumpkin pattern, page 207
❑ yellow and green fabric paint in squeeze bottles
❑ pin backs
❑ craft glue, or glue gun and glue stick

Preparation

Use the pattern on page 207 to cut one pumpkin from orange craft foam for each child.

What to Do

1. Show how to glue the pin to the back of a pumpkin. (Note: If you want the children to be able to wear them immediately, a glue gun will provide the best results. Only adults should use the glue gun.)

2. Using fabric paint, help the children paint eyes, noses, mouths and stems onto their pumpkins.

3. Say, **In the fall, pumpkins are ready to be picked, or harvested. Jesus talked about harvest. He said, The harvest is plentiful, but the workers are few. Jesus meant that many people are ready to hear about His love but there are just a few people spreading the good news. Who can you tell about the love of Jesus?**

Stuffed Fish *Ages 5-12*

Bible Reference: The Miraculous Catch, John 21:3-6

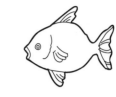

Overview
The children will make 3-D fish that can be used in the "Fishing in the Sea of Galilee" game, or taken home.

Helpers: 1
• one for every 4-5 children

Materials
❑ brown grocery bags
❑ fish pattern, page 209
❑ heavy weight paper or poster board
❑ pencils
❑ scissors
❑ newspaper
❑ stapler
❑ markers
❑ prize tickets
❑ tape

Preparation
Enlarge the fish pattern on heavy weight paper or poster board.

What to Do

1. Have the children trace the pattern on a grocery bag then cut out two identical fish. (Make sure any printing on the grocery bag is on the inside of the fish.)

2. Show how to staple the two shapes together but leave an opening through which to stuff the crumpled newspaper. Finish stapling.

3. Allow the children to color the bag with markers.

4. Ask the children if they are willing to give the fish they have made for use in the "Fishing in the Sea of Galilee" game on page 31. If they are, tape a prize ticket to the fish's mouth. If they want to keep their fish, do not tape a prize ticket to it.

5. Explain that fishermen at the Sea of Galilee used nets, not fishing poles. Say, **There was a time when the fishermen had fished all night and didn't catch anything. Jesus came along and told them to throw the nets into the water again. Peter said, "We haven't caught anything all night, but because You tell us to try again, we will." When the fishermen put the net in because Jesus told them to, they caught so many fish that their nets began to break and the weight of the fish in the boat caused it to almost sink!**

Puzzles

City of Jericho Dot-To-Dot *Ages 5-8*

Bible Reference: City of Jericho, Joshua 6:2-5

Overview
The children connect the dots, forming the city of Jericho

Helpers: 1
• one to distribute materials and supervise

Materials
❑ puzzle page 211
❑ crayons or non-permanent markers

What to Do
1. Reproduce the coloring page for each child.
2. Distribute crayons or markers.
3. Ask the children to connect the dots to form the city.
4. They may color the page when the dots have been connected.
5. Say, **In Bible times every city had enormous walls surrounding it. This kept enemies out.**

Coded Message *Ages 8-12*

Bible Reference: The Good Samaritan, Luke 10:25-37

Overview

The children decipher the code and read the Bible passage.

Helpers: 1

• one to distribute materials andsupervise

Materials

❑ puzzle page 213
❑ pencils

What to Do

1. Make a copy of the coded message for each child.
2. Give a copy of the puzzle and a pencil to each child.
3. Make sure the children understand that each symbol stands for a different letter. Let the children decipher the message.
4. Ask the children to recall the story of the Good Samaritan. Ask, **Who treated the hurt man in a kind and caring way? What did the caring man do?**

Answer: Do to others as you would have them do to you.

David and Goliath *Ages 3-5*

Bible Reference: David and Goliath, 1 Samuel 17:1-50

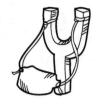

Overview

The children will find the giant, put an "x" on his forehead and color the page.

Helpers: 1

• one to distribute materials and supervise

Materials

❑ page 215
❑ crayons or non-permanent markers
❑ fabric scraps, yarn or ribbon (optional)
❑ glue (optional)

What to Do

1. Reproduce page 215 for each child.
2. Give each child a coloring page and crayons or markers.
3. Ask, **Can you find the giant on this page? The Bible tells us his name was Goliath.**
4. Briefly retell the Bible story of David and Goliath and then suggest that the children make a mark on the giant's forehead where David's stone hit.
5. Encourage the children to color the rest of the page.
6. If you wish, provide fabric scraps, pieces of yarn, ribbon and other materials to glue to the figures.

Find the Sheep's Twin Ages 5-8

Bible Reference: The Parable of the Lost Sheep, Luke 15:4-6

Overview

The children will find the pairs of sheep that are the same, then color the page.

Helpers: 1

• one to distribute materials and supervise

Materials

❑ puzzle, page 217
❑ crayons or non-permanent markers

What to Do

1. Reproduce the coloring page for each child.
2. Distribute crayons or markers to the children.
3. Ask the children to find the two sheep that are alike. Suggest they color the pairs the same.
4. As they are working, briefly explain that Jesus told a parable of the lost sheep. Say, **A parable is a story that teaches a lesson. Jesus told a parable about sheep because in that day, everyone knew what it took to raise sheep. It was a story everyone would understand.**

Note: This page can be used as a backdrop pattern for the game Lost Sheep.

Answer Key

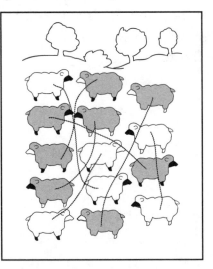

Fruit of the Spirit Word Search *Ages 8-12*

Bible Reference: The Fruits of the Spirit, Galatians 5:22-23

Overview

The children will find the characteristics of a Christian life known as the fruit of the Spirit. Words will be vertical, horizontal and diagonal.

Helpers: 1

• one to distribute materials and supervise

Materials

❑ puzzle page 219
❑ pencil

What to Do

1. Reproduce the puzzle page for each child.
2. Make sure each child has a pencil.
3. Ask the children to circle the hidden words listed below the puzzle.
4. Discuss each characteristic with the children.

Answer Key

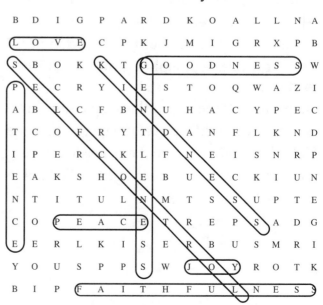

How Do They Grow? *Ages 5-8*

Bible Reference: Isaiah 61:11

Overview
The children color the pictures and cut them apart, then they put the pumpkin pictures in sequence.

Helpers: 1
• one to distribute materials and supervise

Materials
❑ puzzle page 221
❑ crayons or markers
❑ scissors
❑ 8¹/2" x 11" paper
❑ stapler

What to Do
1. Reproduce puzzle page 221 for each child.
2. Distribute scissors and crayons or markers.
3. Allow the children to color the page.
4. Have the children cut out the six rectangles.
5. Ask, **How does a pumpkin grow?** Discuss how God causes plants to grow and the seasons to change.
6. Help the children to put the six pictures in the correct order.
7. Show how to fold a piece of paper in half and cut the page into two equal pieces.
8. Help the children staple the pages together.
9. Have them create a cover page for the booklet on the outside sheet.

How Many Bees? *Ages 4-7*

Bible Reference: The Beatitudes, Matthew 5:3-11

Overview
The children will count the bees, then color them.

Helpers: 1
• one to distribute materials and supervise

Materials
❑ puzzle, page 223
❑ crayons or non-permanent markers

What to Do
1. Reproduce the puzzle page for each child.
2. Give each child a coloring page and crayons or markers.
3. Help each child count the number of bees. Say, **"Bee" is the first sound in the word Beatitudes.**
4. As the children color the page, discuss the beatitudes. Say, **Jesus preached a sermon where He talked about who would be blessed. We call that list the Beatitudes. There are eight Beatitudes.** (Read them from the coloring page.)

Note: This page can be used as a backdrop pattern for the craft "Buzzin' Bees" on page 49.

Answer: 22 bees

Mark Out *Ages 8-12*

Bible Reference: Light of the World, Matthew 5:14-16

Overview
The children will find the hidden Bible verse.

Helpers: 1
- one to distribute materials and supervise

Materials
- ❏ puzzle, page 225
- ❏ pencils

What to Do
1. Reproduce the puzzle page for each child.
2. As the children arrive, give each a copy of the puzzle and a pencil.
3. Have the children mark out the first two letters and circle the third. Continue with this pattern throughout the puzzle.
4. After circling every third letter, the children should copy the circled letters to the blanks below.

ANSWER: In the same way, let your light shine before men, that they may see your good deeds and praise your Father in heaven.

Ten Plagues Crossword *Ages 8-12*

Bible Reference: Exodus 7:14-11:10

Overview

The children will complete the crossword puzzle.

Helpers: 1

• one to distribute materials and supervise

Materials

❑ puzzle page 227
❑ pencil
❑ crayons (optional)

What to Do

1. Reproduce the crossword puzzle for each child.
2. Give each child a copy and a pencil. Have crayons available.
3. Have the children complete the crossword puzzle.
4. The children may color the pictures if they wish.
5. Ask, **Why did God send the plagues?** (He wanted to convince Pharaoh to free the Hebrew people.)

ANSWER KEY

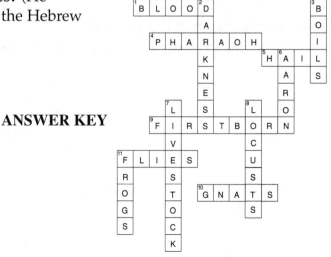

What's Missing? *Ages 3-5*

Bible Reference: Daniel and the Lions' Den, Daniel 6:16-24

Overview

The children will draw the missing lions and color the rest of the page.

Helpers: 1

• one to distribute materials and supervise

Materials

❑ puzzle page 229
❑ crayons or non-permanent markers

What to Do

1. Reproduce the puzzle page for each child.
2. Give each child a coloring page and crayons or markers.
3. Briefly tell the story of Daniel being thrown into the lion's den because he would not obey the king's order to quit praying to God.
4. Ask, **What is missing from this picture?**
5. Encourage the children to draw several lions and then color the rest of the page.

Snacks

Animal Cut-Out Cookies Ages 3-12

Bible Reference: Noah and the Ark, Genesis 6–8

Overview
Roll out the cookie dough and use cookie cutters to make animal shapes.

Helpers: 1
• one for every 3-4 children

Materials
❑ sugar cookie recipe (below)
❑ pastry board
❑ animal-shaped cookie cutters
❑ baking sheets
❑ oven
❑ cooking spray
❑ frosting tubes, if desired

What to Do
Note: If children are helping, instruct them to wash hands before preparing food.
1. Prepare cookie dough in advance by creaming together shortening and sugar. Add vanilla. Beat in egg until light and fluffy. Stir in milk. Sift together dry ingredients then stir into creamed sugar and shortening mixture. Chill one hour or more.
2. Let the children help roll the cookie dough on a floured pastry board.
3. The children should choose a cookie cutter to cut the rolled dough into animal shapes.
4. Bake on greased cookie sheet in 375° oven for 6-8 minutes.
5. As the cookies bake, have the children help clean up and talk about the various Bible stories that have animals (Creation, Noah and the Ark, etc.). Ask, **Who made the animals?**
6. Allow the cookies to cool one minute before removing from pan.
7. Decorate with tubes of frosting, if desired.

Sugar Cookie Recipe
2/3 cup shortening
3/4 cup granulated sugar
1 teaspoon vanilla
1 egg
4 teaspoons milk
2 cups sifted flour
1 1/2 teaspoons baking powder
1/4 teaspoon salt

Variation: Find other cookie cutters to make a snack that reinforces other Bible stories.
Fish for Jonah.
Lion for Daniel.
Butterfly for new life.
Pumpkin or leaves for fall.

Building Blocks *Ages 4-12*

Bible Reference: Joshua 6

Overview

Make building blocks with pretzel sticks and cheese cubes.

Helpers: 1

• one for every 5-6 children

Materials

❑ pretzel sticks
❑ soft cheese cubes
❑ paper plates

What to Do

1. Show the children how to insert a pretzel stick into the center of a cheese cube, putting the materials together like building blocks.

2. Ask, **Can you make a wall like Jericho had?**

Butterfly Pizzas *Ages 3-12*

Bible Reference: New Life, Romans 6:4

Overview
Make miniature pizzas.

Helpers: 1
• one for every 3-4 children

Materials
❑ aluminum foil
❑ permanent marker
❑ refrigerator biscuits
❑ table knives
❑ pizza sauce
❑ teaspoons
❑ shredded mozzarella cheese
❑ meat or vegetable toppings
❑ baking sheet
❑ paper plates
❑ oven

What to Do

Note: If children are helping, instruct them to wash hands before preparing food.

1. Give each child a square of aluminum foil, approximately 6" x 6".
2. Print the child's name on the foil with a permanent marker.
3. Show the children how to pat a single refrigerator biscuit to make it flatter and bigger.
4. Help them cut the flattened biscuit in half.
5. Show how to move the left half of the biscuit to the right side of the other half, keeping both halves on the aluminum foil. Cut edges will both be on the outside (see illustration at right).

6. Allow the children to spread a teaspoon of pizza sauce on each half.
7. Let them top the pizzas with shredded cheese and any other topping they wish.
8. Slide the butterfly pizzas (still on foil squares) onto a baking sheet.
9. Bake in 400° oven for 10 minutes. Serve hot.
10. Explain that the butterfly is a symbol of new life. say, **The butterfly makes me think about spring and new life. When someone believes that Jesus is God's Son and says they need God's help to live the right way, they have new life. They will live that new life in Heaven with Jesus some day.**

75

Cheese Coins Ages 3-12

Bible Reference: The Parable of the Coins, Luke 15:8-10

Overview
Mix cheese dough, then cut and bake it.

Helpers: 1
• one for every 3-4 children

Materials
❑ 1/2 teaspoon salt
❑ pinch of baking soda
❑ 1/4 teaspoon garlic salt
❑ 1 cup white flour
❑ 1/4 cup shortening
❑ 3-4 tablespoons of water
❑ 1/2 cup finely shredded
    cheddar cheese
❑ bowl
❑ spoon
❑ rolling pin
❑ pastry board
❑ plastic milk jug lids
❑ baking sheet
❑ oven
❑ cooking spray

What to Do
Note: If children are helping, instruct them to wash hands before preparing food.

1. Have the children add premeasured flour, salt, baking powder and garlic salt, then help stir it together.
2. Cut in shortening.
3. Stir in cheese.
4. Add just enough water to combine flour and shortening.
5. Let the children take turns kneading the dough until everything is combined.
6. Roll the dough on a floured pastry board to slightly less than 1/4 inch in thickness.
7. Help the children use a milk jug lid to cut the dough into coins. Dip the lid into flour to keep the dough from sticking.
8. Place the coins on a lightly greased baking sheet.
9. Bake in a 350° oven for 10 minutes. The recipes makes 24-30 coins.
10. Retell the parable of the lost coin as the coins bake and the children help clean up. Say, **Jesus told a story about a woman who had ten silver coins, but lost one. She cleaned her house, searching everywhere until she found it. Then she called her friends and neighbors and said, Rejoice with me. Jesus said the angels rejoice even more when one lost person tells God they are sorry for the way he or she has lived. Just like the one coin was important to the woman, each person is important to God.**

Elephant Trunks *Ages 3-12*

Bible Reference: Noah and the Ark, Genesis 7:14-15

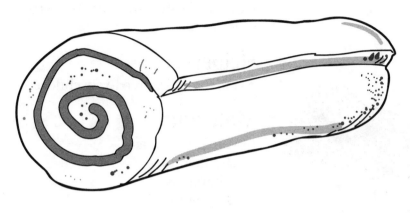

Overview
Make an open-faced peanut butter and jelly sandwich and roll it up.

Helpers: 1
• one for every 3-4 children

Materials
❑ bread
❑ table knives
❑ peanut butter
❑ jelly
❑ paper plates

What to Do
Note: If children are helping, instruct them to wash hands before preparing food.
1. Trim the crust from the bread.
2. Help the children spread peanut butter on one piece of bread.
3. Add a layer of jelly.
4. Show how to roll the bread jellyroll-style (see illustration).
5. As the children enjoy their snacks, talk about the unusual features some animals have. Ask, **Why do you think God gave the elephant a trunk?**

Fruit Kebabs and Dip *Ages 3-12*

Bible Reference: Fruit of the Spirit, Galatians 5:22

Overview
Cut up fresh fruit into bite-size pieces.

Helpers: 1
• one for every five to six children

Materials
fresh fruit such as:
- ❑ pineapples
- ❑ bananas
- ❑ apples
- ❑ tangerines
- ❑ strawberries
- ❑ plastic knives
- ❑ lemon juice
- ❑ one 8-oz. package of cream cheese
- ❑ one 7-oz. jar of marshmallow creme
- ❑ 2-3 tablespoons of cherry juice
- ❑ toothpicks

What to Do
Note: If children are helping, instruct them to wash hands before preparing food.

1. Blend together the cream cheese, marshmallow creme and cherry juice.
2. Let the children take turns stirring the mixture. Chill.
3. Let the children help cut the fruit into bite-size pieces.
4. Banana and apple slices may be dipped in lemon juice or orange juice to prevent browning.
5. Show the children how to slide pieces onto a toothpick or shish kebab skewer.
6. Serve the fruit with the dip. Encourage the children to eat the fruit as soon as it is assembled.
7. Ask, **Have you ever heard of the fruit of the Spirit? These are traits that come to us when we invite Jesus to live in us. Can you name any of the characteristics?** (Love, joy, peace, gentleness, kindness, goodness, patience, faithfulness and self-control.) **There are nine characteristics called the fruit of the Spirit. Who can tell me a way to show love?** (joy, peace, patience, kindness, goodness, faithfulness, gentleness and self-control.)

Giant Pretzels *Ages 3-12*

Bible Reference: David and Goliath, 1 Samuel 17:4

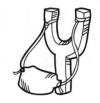

Overview
Shape the dough into soft pretzels.

Helpers: 1
• one for every 3-4 children

Materials
❑ large bowl
❑ spoon
❑ two packages of dry yeast
❑ one tablespoon sugar
❑ two cups of warm water
❑ one teaspoon salt
❑ five cups of flour
❑ two teaspoons of baking soda
❑ water
❑ medium bowl
❑ coarse salt
❑ baking sheet
❑ oven
❑ cooking spray

What to Do
Note: If children are helping, instruct them to wash hands before preparing food.

1. Before the party, mix the dough. Let the yeast and sugar dissolve in $1^1/_2$ cups of warm (110–115°) water.
2. Stir in salt and flour.
3. Knead until the texture is soft and smooth.
4. Let the dough rise 20–60 minutes.
5. Separate the dough into eighteen pieces of equal size.
6. Give each child one piece of dough to roll into a long, narrow snake-like shape.
7. Help the children form the length of the dough into a pretzel shape.
8. In a medium bowl, dissolve the baking soda in a $1/_2$-cup of warm water.
9. Dip each pretzel into the soda-water mixture.
10. Sprinkle on coarse salt.
11. Bake on a greased baking sheet for 17-20 minutes in a 425° oven. Allow the pretzels to cool before the children eat them.
12. Ask, **Do you know what giant means? These are giant pretzels. Can you think of any Bible story that includes a giant?** (David and Goliath) **David and Goliath had a fight. Who won?** (David) **Who do you think would win a fight between a teenage boy and a giant?** (the giant) **Who helped David win the fight?** (God)

Lion Crackers *Ages 3-12*

Bible Reference: Daniel and the Lions' Den, Daniel 6

Overview

The children will make a snack cracker.

Helpers: 1

• one for every 10 children

Materials

❑ round snack crackers
❑ peanut butter
❑ plastic knives
❑ brown mini M&M® baking chips
❑ carrots
❑ black licorice strings
❑ paper plates
❑ food processor

Preparation

You will need one snack cracker, three mini M&M's® and two licorice strings per child.

What to Do

Note: If children are helping, instruct them to wash hands before preparing food.

1. Julienne the carrots.

2. Show how to coat one side of the cracker with peanut butter.

3. Demonstrate how to use mini M&M's® to make eyes and a nose.

4. Show how to use licorice strings to make whiskers.

5. Help the children arrange julienne carrot sticks around the edge to make a mane.

6. As the children eat ask, **Who remembers a Bible story that has lions?**

Rainbow on a Cloud _Ages 3-12_

Bible Reference: Noah and the Ark, Genesis 9:12-16

Overview

The children place M&M's® on a frosting-covered graham cracker in the shape of a rainbow.

Helpers: 1

• one for every five to six children

Materials

❑ graham crackers
❑ prepared white frosting
❑ M&M's® in shallow containers
❑ table knives or craft sticks

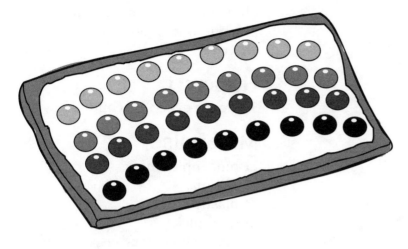

What to Do

Note: If children are helping, instruct them to wash hands before preparing food.

1. Have a completed cracker on display.

2. First, show the children how to cover the surface of the graham cracker with frosting.

3. Allow them to make a rainbow from M&M's® on the cracker.

4. Suggest that children begin with the red M&M's® and form an arch across the cracker. (Red is the top color in a rainbow.)

5. As the children eat ask, **Why did God put a rainbow in the sky?** (As a reminder of His promise.)

Shining Candle *Ages 5-12*

Bible Reference: Light of the World, Matthew 5:16

Overview
Stand half a banana inside a pineapple ring and top it with a cherry.

Helpers: 1
• one for every 2-3 children

Materials
❑ pineapple rings
❑ bananas
❑ plastic knives
❑ toothpicks
❑ maraschino cherries
❑ paper plates

Preparation
You will need half of a banana, one cherry and one pineapple ring per child.

What to Do
Note: If the children are helping, instruct them to wash hands before preparing food.

1. Let the children place a pineapple ring on a small paper plate.
2. Show how to cut the curved end off of the top end of the banana.
3. Explain where to insert a maraschino cherry onto a toothpick and stick it in the top of the banana.
4. Show how to stand half a banana in the middle of the pineapple ring.
5. As the children are assembling the candle and eating it ask, **Who said I am the light of the world?** (Jesus) **What did He mean?** (That He came to teach us how to live our lives. The way Jesus lived His life is an example for us that lights our paths.)

Special Catch Snack Ages 3-12

Bible Reference: Fishers of Men, Matthew 4:18-20

Overview

The children will help prepare and eat the snack.

Helpers: 1

• one for every ten children

Materials

❑ large bowl
❑ spoon
❑ 12-oz. paper or plastic cups
❑ two cups of cheddar cheese goldfish crackers
❑ two cups of pretzel goldfish crackers
❑ two cups of parmesan goldfish crackers
❑ one cup of raisins
❑ one cup of M&M's®
❑ one cup of peanuts
❑ one cup of candy corn
❑ one cup of dried banana chips
❑ one cup of red hots

What to Do

Note: If children are helping, instruct them to wash hands before preparing food.

1. Let each child add one premeasured ingredient.
2. Mix together all of the ingredients in a large bowl.
3. The children can serve themselves by scooping a cupful from the bowl.
4. The recipe makes approximately 30 3-oz. servings.
5. Say, **Jesus said He would make Simon Peter and Andrew fishers of men. What did Jesus mean?** (Jesus wanted the brothers to help others find God.)

Zebra Brownies Ages 3-12

Bible Reference: Noah and the Ark, Genesis 7:14-15

Overview
Help prepare the brownies and enjoy!

Helpers: 1
• one per batch

Materials
❑ family-size brownie mix with ingredients listed on box
❑ two 3-oz. packages of cream cheese, softened
❑ two tablespoons of margarine or butter, softened
❑ 1/3 cup of sugar
❑ two eggs
❑ two tablespoons flour
❑ 1/4 teaspoon vanilla
❑ 9" x 13" baking pan
❑ electric mixer
❑ table knife
❑ cooking spray
❑ large bowl

What to Do
Note: If children are helping, instruct them to wash hands before preparing food.

1. The brownie batter may be made in advance or with the help of two or three children.
2. Ask one child to grease a 9" x 13" pan.
3. Blend together the cream cheese and margarine with electric mixer.
4. Let the children add the measured sugar, flour and vanilla.
5. Add eggs.
6. Beat until smooth. Set aside.
7. Prepare brownie mix according to package directions.
8. Put half of the brownie batter into a prepared 9" x 13" pan.
9. Spread all of the cream cheese mixture over the brownie batter.
10. Spoon the rest of the brownie batter in dollops on top of the cream cheese mixture.
11. A child can "marble" the brownies by pulling a table knife through the chocolate and white mixtures with gentle swirls.
12. Bake in a 350° oven for 36-39 minutes.
13. Cool before cutting.
14. Makes 15 large brownies.

Costumes

Animals (Basic Animal Body) Ages 2-12

Bible Reference: Noah and the Ark, Genesis 7:1-3

Materials

- ❑ brown paper grocery bag
- ❑ several plastic shopping bags or colored trash bags or crepe paper
- ❑ scissors
- ❑ clear tape
- ❑ felt
- ❑ 2" width of felt long enough to fit around child's head
- ❑ ear patterns
- ❑ face paint

What to Do

1. To make the body of the animal cut a straight line up the center of a brown paper grocery bag.
2. Cut a neck opening and two armholes (see illustration at right).
3. For the animal's fur, fringe the plastic shopping bags from the open end. Stop cutting 2"-3" from the bottom of the sack (see illustration at right).
4. Tape the plastic bags to the paper bag overlapping the fringe (see illustration at right).
5. The grocery bag can be covered in other ways. It may be painted or pieces of crepe paper can be glued to the bag.
6. Create the animal's ears by first making a headband from 2"-wide felt.
7. Pin or glue the headband to fit the child's head.
8. Cut out an appropriate pair of animal ears and glue or staple them to the headband, using the patterns on pages 231 to 233.
9. Add a nose or face paint and a tail to complete the costume. See ideas on the following pages for specific animals.

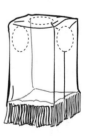

Beagle (Dog) *Ages 2-12*

Materials

- ❑ basic animal body
- ❑ collar
- ❑ felt, crepe paper or jumbo chenille wire
- ❑ tan, brown or black sweat suit
- ❑ pattern for ears on page 233

What to Do

1. Make the basic animal body using the directions on page 87. Use the dog ear pattern on page 233.
2. Using brown face paint, paint a large irregular shape on one side   of the child's face to resemble a spotted dog (see illustration).
3. Paint the nose brown or black and add whiskers.
4. Add a collar to make it a pet beagle.
5. Complete the costume by attaching a tail made from felt, crepe paper or jumbo chenille wire to a tan, brown or black sweat suit.

Cat *Ages 2-12*

Materials

- ❑ basic animal body
- ❑ felt, crepe paper or jumbo chenille wire
- ❑ sweat suit
- ❑ collar
- ❑ pattern for ears on page 233

What to Do

1. Make the basic animal body using the directions on page 87. Use the cat ear pattern on page 233.
2. Use face paint to paint a small pink or black circle on the end of the child's nose (see illustration).
3. Paint several small dots on the child's cheeks. Draw a whisker from each dot.
4. Complete the costume by attaching a tail made from felt, crepe paper or jumbo loopy chenille to an appropriately colored sweat suit.
5. Add a collar to make it a pet cat!

COW *Ages 2-12*

Materials

- ❑ basic animal body
- ❑ black felt
- ❑ white sweat suit
- ❑ glue
- ❑ felt, crepe paper or jumbo chenille wire
- ❑ pattern for ears on page 233

What to Do

1. Make the basic animal body using the directions on page 87. Use the cow ear pattern on page 233.
2. Using face paint, color large, black irregular shapes on the child's face.
3. Cut irregular shapes from black felt to make spots. Glue then onto a white sweat suit.
4. Add a tail made from felt, crepe paper or jumbo chenille wire to complete the costume.

Note: You can also use a black sweat suit with white spots.

Elephant *Ages 2-12*

Materials

- ❏ basic animal body
- ❏ pattern for ears on page 231
- ❏ gray construction paper or felt
- ❏ cardboard egg carton
- ❏ gray paint
- ❏ paintbrushes
- ❏ glue
- ❏ hole punch
- ❏ yarn or elastic
- ❏ black yarn
- ❏ gray sweat suit

What to Do

1. Make the basic animal body using the directions on page 87. Use the elephant ear pattern on page 231.
2. To make a trunk, cut apart a cardboard egg carton, producing 12 individual cups.
3. Glue the cups together, one on top the other and in a slightly curved fashion to make a trunk (see illustration).
4. Punch tiny holes on each side of the trunk to attach either yarn or a thin piece of elastic to the trunk.
5. Paint the trunk gray and allow to dry.
6. Position the trunk over the child's nose and tie it in place, adjusting it to fit the head comfortably.
7. A black yarn tail attached to gray pants or sweat suit will complete the costume.

Koala Bear *Ages 2-12*

Materials

- ❑ basic animal body
- ❑ ear pattern on page 231
- ❑ tan construction paper
- ❑ tan pom-pom
- ❑ gray or brown sweat suit

What to Do

1. Make the basic animal body using the directions on page 87.
2. Use the ear pattern on page 231 to cut two from tan construction paper.
3. To complete the costume, use face paint and paint a large oval shaped nose on the child's nose. Paint on whiskers.
4. A large tan pom-pom attached to the seat of a gray or brown sweat suit will complete the costume.

Lion *Ages 2-12*

Materials

- ❑ basic animal body
- ❑ paper plate
- ❑ orange, brown or tan paint
- ❑ string or elastic
- ❑ stapler
- ❑ clear tape
- ❑ pattern for lion ears on page 231
- ❑ brown construction paper or felt
- ❑ glue
- ❑ chenille wire or yarn
- ❑ brown, tan or orange sweat suit
- ❑ paintbrush

What to Do

1. Make the basic animal body using the directions on page 87.
   Do not make the headband.
2. Paint a paper plate orange, brown or tan for the lion's mane.
3. Cut out the center of the plate, making the hole large enough to fit the child's face through it.
4. Cut slits all around the plate to fringe it (see illustration).
5. Staple string or elastic at either side of the mane to wrap around the head and hold in place. Cover the staples with tape to avoid injury.
6. Use the pattern on page 231 to make the lion ears from brown construction paper or felt. Glue them to the paper plate.
7. Pin a tail made from loopy chenille wire or yarn to a brown, tan or orange sweat suit to complete the costume.

Pig *Ages 2-12*

Materials

- ❑ basic animal body
- ❑ 3-oz. unwaxed paper cup
- ❑ pink paint
- ❑ paint brush
- ❑ black marker
- ❑ hole punch
- ❑ yarn or elastic
- ❑ chenille wire
- ❑ pink sweat suit

What to Do

1. Make the basic animal body using the directions on page 87. Use the pig ear pattern on page 233.
2. To make a pig nose, use a 3-oz. unwaxed paper cup.
3. Trim the cup to be $1^1/_2$" tall.
4. Paint the cup pink.
5. Using a black marker, draw two nostrils on the end of the cup.
6. Punch a small hole on each side of the cup and attach yarn or elastic.
7. Position the cup over the child's nose and adjust it to fit. Note: You may need to cut a small wedge shape from the bottom of the cup to allow for better breathing.
8. Attach a small curled chenille wire to the seat of a pink sweat suit to complete the costume.

Bee *Ages 3-10*

Bible Reference: The Beatitudes, Matthew 5:3-11

Materials

- ❑ two sheets of yellow poster board
- ❑ two 2" x 8" strips of black felt
- ❑ two black chenille wires
- ❑ two $1/2$" black pom-poms
- ❑ 2" x 25" strip of black felt
- ❑ black sweat suit
- ❑ black marker
- ❑ glue or Velcro®
- ❑ black poster board
- ❑ black gloves

What to Do

1. Cut two large ovals from the yellow poster board to be the front and back of the bee's body (Adjust the size according to the size of the child.)
2. Glue or staple the 2" x 8 strips of felt to the poster board body as shoulder straps.
3. Color wide stripes with a black marker on both sides of the body.
4. To make the antennae, fit the 2" wide strip of felt around the head.
5. Cut to fit and glue or Velcro® it.
6. Glue one pom-pom to the top of each chenille wire.
7. Slide one chenille wire inside the headband near each temple.
8. Fold the black poster board in half and draw half of the bee wings (see illustration at right). Cut them out.
9. Dress the child in a black sweat suit.
10. Fit the bee body over the child's shoulders.
11. Attach the wings to the back of the body using glue or Velcro®.
12. Add black gloves to complete the costume.

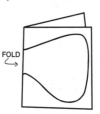

FOLD

Bible Characters *Ages 3-Adult*

Bible Reference: David and Goliath, 1 Samuel 17:1-50

Materials
❑ one large pillowcase
❑ scissors
❑ rope

What to Do
1. Cut a neck hole in the top center of the pillowcase.
2. Cut arm holes in the sides (see illustration).
3. Wrap a piece of rope or twine around the waist to make a belt.
4. The child can be barefoot or wear sandals (see Bible Sandal directions on page 97).

Variations
For a shepherd, add a large stick or staff.
For David, add a sling shot to the wardrobe.
For Mary, wrap a blue cloth around the head.
For someone who is wealthier, add a sash across the shoulder and tuck it into the belt.
For one of the disciples, add a beard.

Bible Sandals *Ages 3 and up*

Bible Reference: David and Goliath, 1 Samuel 17:1-50

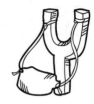

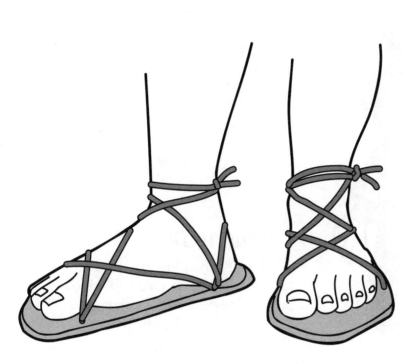

Materials

- ❑ two pieces of cardboard
- ❑ piece of vinyl or leather
- ❑ leather lacing
- ❑ pen or marker
- ❑ hole punch
- ❑ scissors

What to Do

1. Trace around the person's feet and cut footprint shapes from cardboard.

2. Using the cardboard for sizing and the illustration as a guide, cut the sandal shape from vinyl or leather.

3. Punch two holes on each side of the top of the sandal.

4. Punch one hole on each side of the heel (see illustration).

5. Glue the cardboard inside the vinyl to provide stability.

6. Thread lacing through the holes.

7. Use a criss-cross pattern to tie the lacing at the ankle.

Bread of Life *Ages 3-12*

Bible Reference: John 6:35

Materials

- ❑ two pieces of stiff cardboard, approximately 22" x 22"
- ❑ two 24" pieces of 1¹/₂" white ribbon
- ❑ four 12" pieces of 1¹/₂" white ribbon
- ❑ hot glue gun or duct tape
- ❑ polyester batting
- ❑ bread pattern on page 235
- ❑ brown spray paint
- ❑ brown sweatsuit

What to Do

1. Use the glue gun or duct tape to attach each 24" piece of ribbon to the cardboard to form the shoulder straps.
2.. Attach 12" pieces to the sides for ties.
3. Enlarge the pattern on page 235 to child size. Cut the batting into the shape of a slice of bread. See page 13 for enlargement instructions.
4. Use the brown spray paint on the edges to make them look like bread crusts.
5. Glue the batting to the outside of the cardboard pieces.
6. Print one of the following phrases on paper and pin it to the costume: Jesus — the bread of life or Man does not live by bread alone.

Butterfly *Ages 3-10*

Materials

- ❑ four wire coat hangers
- ❑ duct tape
- ❑ 70" of ribbon
- ❑ white or colored panty hose
- ❑ brightly-colored fabric
- ❑ hot glue gun
- ❑ 1" wide black elastic
- ❑ safety pin
- ❑ two long chenille wires

What to Do

1. Begin with a black sweat suit or a black leotard and tights.
2. Make the butterfly wings by twisting together the handles of two coat hangers.
3. Repeat with the second set of coat hangers.
4. Use the duct tape to bind the two sets together at the twisted end.

5. Pull and bend the coat hangers to form a pair of wings with upper and lower sections.
6. Stretch white or colored panty hose over the wings.
7. Hot glue brightly colored fabric to the wings.
8. Using two 32" pieces of ribbon, make two large loops by gluing or pinning the ends together.
9. Attach the loops to the wings with a 6" piece of ribbon.
10. To wear the wings, put one arm through each loop. Adjust the fit by making loops larger or smaller.
11. Make antennae by cutting a length of elastic to fit securely around the person's head.
12. Pin the two ends together.
13. Curl one end of each chenille wire.
14. Slide one chenille wire under the elastic at each temple.

Candle *Ages 3 and up*

Bible Reference: God Is Light, 1 John 1:5

Let
Your
Light
Shine

Materials

❑ two pieces of 22" x 28" poster board, any color
❑ stapler
❑ 36-48" of $1\frac{1}{2}$" wide ribbon
❑ yellow or orange construction paper
❑ flame pattern on page 237
❑ clear tape

What to Do

1. Staple together the two pieces of poster board with a 4" overlap.
2. Staple two to three times near the edge, then again as far as the stapler will reach.
3. Cover the staples with tape to avoid injury.
4. Fit the poster board around the child and staple the other ends together forming a cylinder. Cover the staples with tape.
5. Print on the front of the poster board one of these: I am the light of the world; Let your light shine before men; This little light of mine, I'm gonna let it shine!
6. Measure then cut the ribbon to fit as shoulder straps.
7. For a headpiece, cut a 1" wide strip of construction paper. Staple two pieces together if necessary and fit it around the head, covering the staples with tape.
8. Use the pattern on page 237 and cut a flame from yellow or orange construction paper.
9. Staple the flame to the headband.
10. For a full-length costume, use a long piece of corrugated cardboard instead of the poster board. However, be aware that a full-length costume will restrict movement.

Fisherman *Ages 8 and up*

Bible Reference: The Miraculous Catch, John 21:3-6

Materials

- ❑ 23" x 46" of tan felt
- ❑ felt scraps
- ❑ fabric markers or fabric paint
- ❑ fishing hat, pole or wading boots

What to Do

1. Fold the felt in half, making it 23" x 23", and cut as the illustration shows. (The folded edge becomes the center back and the cut edges form the center front.)

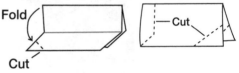

2. Fold each center front to the center back and cut armholes.

3. Adjust to fit a child or adult by making arm holes smaller or larger.

4. To decorate, cut out 3" x 5" pieces from felt remnants and either glue or sew to the vest as pockets. Remember: a fishing vest has lots of pockets all around!

5. Use fabric markers or paint to write captions such as: I am a fisher of men; The Bible is my disciple bait; or I am a follower of Jesus.

6. Add an old fishing hat with fishing lures, a fishing pole, or wading boots to make your costume complete.

Flower *Ages 3-10*

Bible Reference: Jesus' Resurrection and New Life, Romans 6:4

Materials
- ❑ shower cap
- ❑ tissue paper
- ❑ stapler
- ❑ clear tape
- ❑ green sweat suit

What to Do

1. Cut the tissue paper into 12" x 15" lengths. Fold each length in half.
2. Gather the open ends of the folded tissue paper to make this end narrower.
3. Staple the open ends of the folded tissue paper to the elastic band of a shower cap. Cover staples with tape to avoid injury.
4. The cap becomes the center of the flower and the tissue paper the petals. Continue making petals until you have filled the entire edge of the cap.
5. Fluff the tissue paper to make it look like petals around the head. You can size the cap to fit a child's head by using safety pins or sewing a small tuck in the back of the elastic.
6. Dress the child in a green sweat suit and put on the cap to make a flower!

Fruit *Ages 3 and up*

Bible Reference: The Fruit of the Spirit, Galatians 5:22

Materials

- ❑ cardboard
- ❑ paint
- ❑ purple or green balloons (grapes)
- ❑ cap
- ❑ safety pin
- ❑ sweat suit or tights
- ❑ brown crepe paper

What to Do

1. Construct the base for the costume as described for Bread of Life on page 98. Cut the cardboard into the shape of the fruit desired.
2. Spray paint the cardboard the appropriate color.
3. For grapes, attach inflated balloons to the cardboard.
4. Have the child wear a matching sweat suit or tights.
5. Complete the costume with a headpiece. For a grape, pin an inflated balloon to a cap.
6. For other fruit, use a sheet of brown crepe paper to make a stem. Tuck one end of the crepe paper into the collar of the sweatshirt, extending it above the child's head.
7. Twist that end. Leave opening for the child's face.
8. A brown knit hat with a felt leaf pinned on it could also serve as a stem.

Pharaoh *Ages 3 and up*

Bible Reference: God's Plagues on Pharoah, Exodus 7:14-11:10

Materials

- ❏ 18" x 42" piece of fabric
- ❏ 36" circle of fabric
- ❏ 2" x 24" piece of felt
- ❏ straight pins
- ❏ craft paints
- ❏ scissors

What to Do

1. For the headdress, fold the 18" x 42" piece of fabric in half, making it 18" x 21".
2. Using the illustration below as a guide, draw the headdress onto the fabric and cut it out.
3. Decorate the headdress using craft paints. Designs could include stripes, squiggly lines or dots.
4. Fold the headdress in half and mark the mid-point with a pin.
5. Measure the child's head from temple to temple.
6. Make a mark on the headdress at each temple, and cut 2" slits very close to the bottom edge. (Example: If the measurement is 12" from temple to temple, make a mark 6" on each side of the centerline of the headdress.)
7. Make a headband from the 2" x 24" piece of felt by inserting the ends of the headband through the slits of the headdress on the front side of the fabric.
8. Tie the headband around the child's head. The fabric will fall around the head to make a headdress.
9. For neckwear, cut a neck hole in the 36" circle of fabric (see illustration at right). This can be larger or smaller depending on who is wearing it.
10. Lay the fabric flat and decorate it with craft paints, jewels, sequins, glitter paints or fabric crayons. Wait until the paint and glue are dry before allowing the child to put on the costume.

Roman Soldier *Ages 3 and up*

Materials

- ❑ three sheets of gold poster board (22" x 36")
- ❑ helmet and ear piece patterns on pages 241-243
- ❑ 1½" foam ball, painted gold
- ❑ breastplate pattern on page 239
- ❑ two large, gold buttons
- ❑ hot glue gun
- ❑ glue stick
- ❑ skirting pattern on page 245
- ❑ one 2" wide strip of felt
- ❑ stapler
- ❑ clear tape
- ❑ red felt
- ❑ red or blue sweat suit
- ❑ triangle pattern on page 247

What to Do

Helmet

1. Cut one of the sheets of poster board in half, to make two 22" x 18" pieces.
2. Use the pattern on page 243 as a guide to cut two helmet pieces. (Adjust dimensions to accommodate head sizes.) If necessary, follow the directions for enlarging patterns on page 13.
3. Staple the helmet pieces together. Put tape across the bottom of the staples to avoid injury.
4. Use the pattern on page 241 to cut out ear pieces.
5. Glue the ear pieces onto the inside of the helmet (see illustration at right).
6. Attach the gold ball to the top.

Breastplate

1. Fold half of a sheet of poster board in half.
2. Use the pattern on page 239 to draw the breastplate on the poster board (use a larger piece of poster board and the directions on page 13 to make it larger).
3. Hot glue the gold buttons in place. Use caution when using a hot glue gun around children.

Skirting

1. Using the pattern on page 245, cut eight to 10 pieces for the skirting (number will vary for the size of the child).
2. Fit the felt band around the child's waist.
3. Glue or staple the gold pieces to the waistband.
4. Cover any rough edges of staples with tape.

Shield

1. Cut a large circle from one sheet of gold poster board.
2. On the back of the circle, attach handles by making two loops from 2" wide pieces of felt (see illustration above).
3. Use the pattern on page 247 to cut four red felt triangles and glue them to the shield.

Patterns
&
Reproducibles

Volunteer Chart

Committee: _____

Committee Chair: _____

Volunteers	Activity	Hours
_____	_____	_____
_____	_____	_____
_____	_____	_____
_____	_____	_____
_____	_____	_____

Committee: _____

Committee Chair: _____

Volunteers	Activity	Hours
_____	_____	_____
_____	_____	_____
_____	_____	_____
_____	_____	_____

Sample Bulletin Announcements

option #1
Pack Up the Kids
We're Going to Church Saturday Night

Family Fun on Halloween Night can be found at church. From [times] on [date] there will be games, prizes, food, costumes and activities for an evening of family fun. Tickets for one round of activities cost $5. Children dressed as Bible characters will receive special prizes. It will be a fun, safe, family evening for all.

Members of the youth group are staffing the games and are encouraged to attend the planning session at the [date] meeting. Others wishing to help should contact the church office. Simple plans for costumes are located in the narthex.

option #2
[church name] Is the Place to Be Halloween Night

This year we will be offering a fun, safe environment for families of all ages to attend. Bible-based games will be the highlight of the evening along with food, crafts and Bible stories. Children dressed as Bible characters will receive special prizes. Mark your calendars now to attend the Family Fall Festival on [date] from [times].

Pumpkin

Family Postcard

You are invited
to a
Fall Festival!

Where:

When:

Cost:

Invitation

You are invited
to a
Fall Festival!

Where:

When:

Cost:

Pumpkin Table Tent

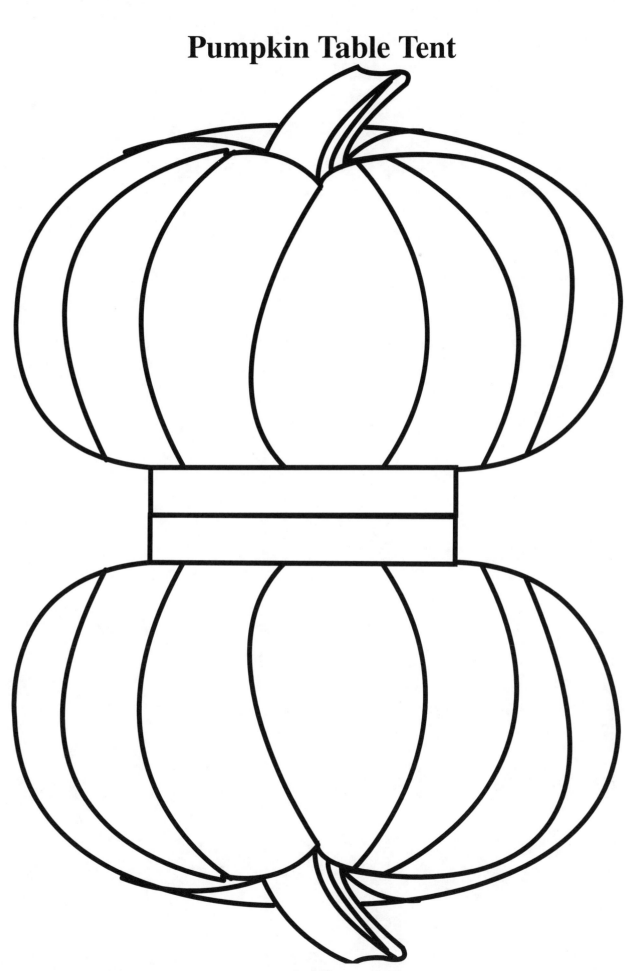

Elongated Leaf Pattern

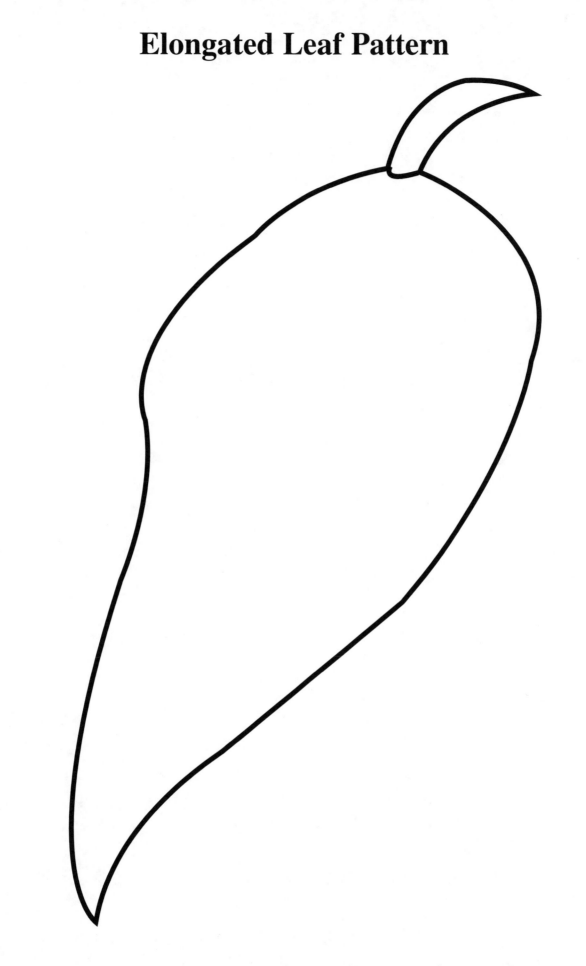

Fodder Shock Pattern

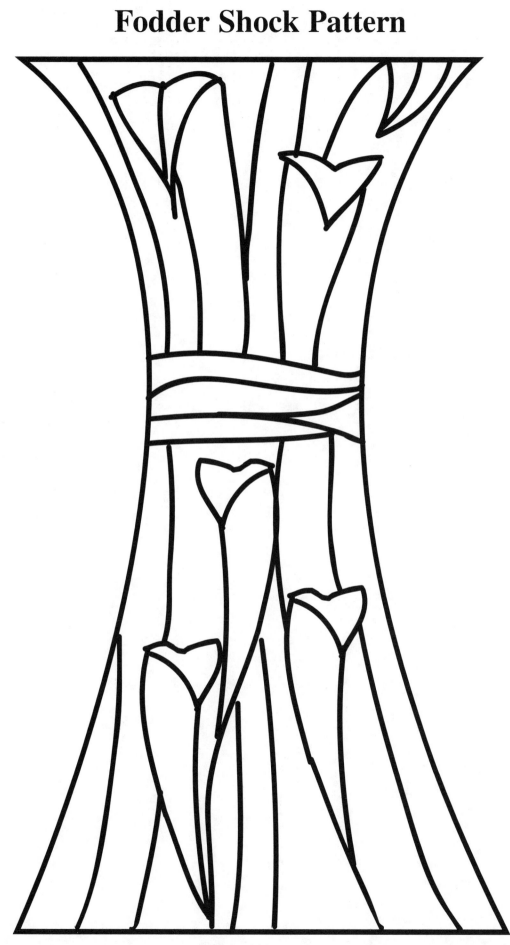

Gourd

Tree Pattern

Owl

Moon & Stars

Registration Form

Welcome! Please fill out the following information, then accompany your child through all of the activities.

Child's Name: _____

Parent or Guardian's Name: _____

Address: _____

_____

Phone Number: _____

Welcome! Please fill out the following information, then accompany your child through all of the activities.

Child's Name: _____

Parent or Guardian's Name: _____

Address: _____

_____

Phone Number: _____

Game Tickets

This ticket is for **1 Game** _____	This ticket is for **1 Game** _____
This ticket is for **1 Game** _____	This ticket is for **1 Game** _____
This ticket is for **1 Game** _____	This ticket is for **1 Game** _____
This ticket is for **1 Game** _____	This ticket is for **1 Game** _____
This ticket is for **1 Game** _____	This ticket is for **1 Game** _____
This ticket is for **1 Game** _____	This ticket is for **1 Game** _____
This ticket is for **1 Game** _____	This ticket is for **1 Game** _____
This ticket is for **1 Game** _____	This ticket is for **1 Game** _____
This ticket is for **1 Story Stop** _____	This ticket is for **1 Story Stop** _____

Snack Tickets

This ticket is for **1 Snack** _____	This ticket is for **1 Snack** _____
This ticket is for **1 Snack** _____	This ticket is for **1 Snack** _____
This ticket is for **1 Snack** _____	This ticket is for **1 Snack** _____
This ticket is for **1 Snack** _____	This ticket is for **1 Snack** _____
This ticket is for **1 Snack** _____	This ticket is for **1 Snack** _____
This ticket is for **1 Snack** _____	This ticket is for **1 Snack** _____
This ticket is for **1 Snack** _____	This ticket is for **1 Snack** _____
This ticket is for **1 Snack** _____	This ticket is for **1 Snack** _____
This ticket is for **1 Snack** _____	This ticket is for **1 Snack** _____

Prize Tickets

This ticket is worth **1 Prize Point**	This ticket is worth **1 Prize Point**
This ticket is worth **1 Prize Point**	This ticket is worth **1 Prize Point**
This ticket is worth **1 Prize Point**	This ticket is worth **1 Prize Point**
This ticket is worth **1 Prize Point**	This ticket is worth **1 Prize Point**
This ticket is worth **1 Prize Point**	This ticket is worth **1 Prize Point**
This ticket is worth **1 Prize Point**	This ticket is worth **1 Prize Point**
This ticket is worth **1 Prize Point**	This ticket is worth **1 Prize Point**
This ticket is worth **1 Prize Point**	This ticket is worth **1 Prize Point**
This ticket is worth **1 Prize Point**	This ticket is worth **1 Prize Point**

Footprint Pattern

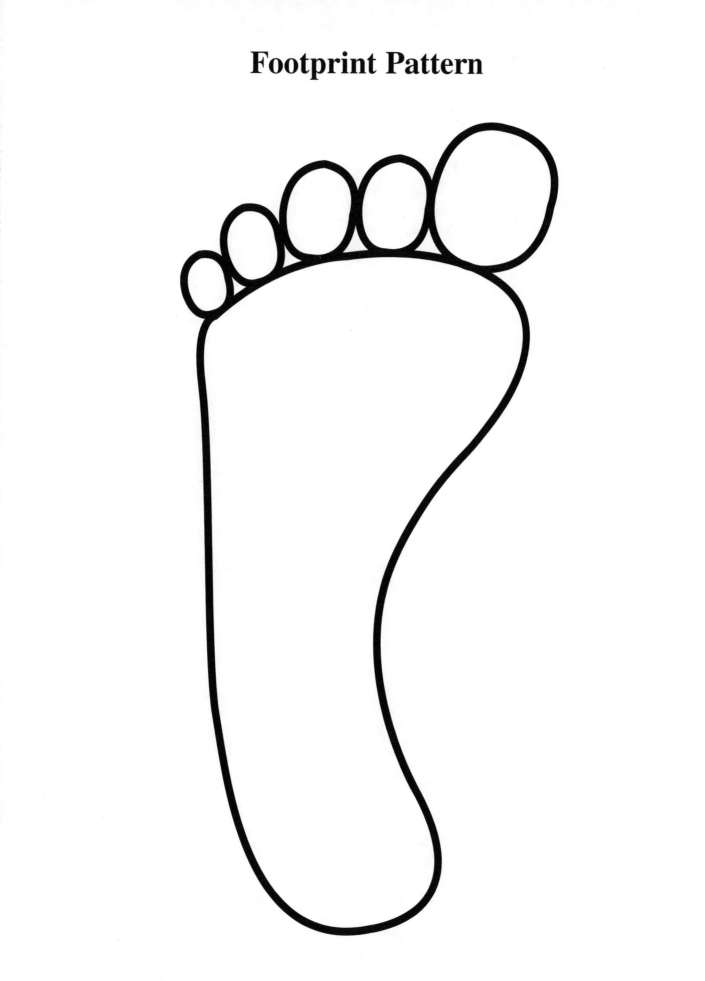

Indian Corn Pattern

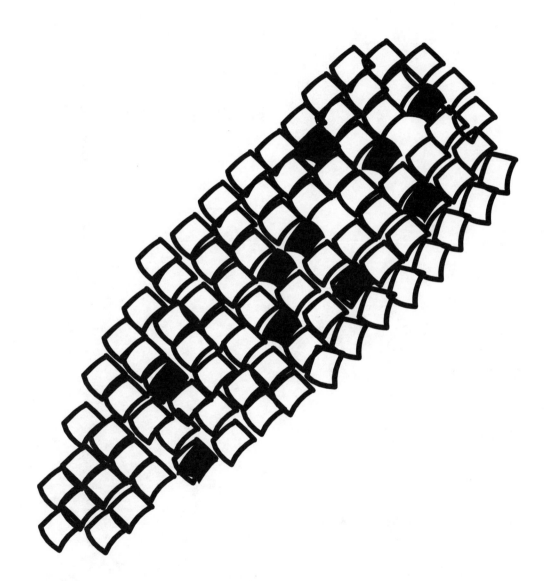

Spiral Pattern

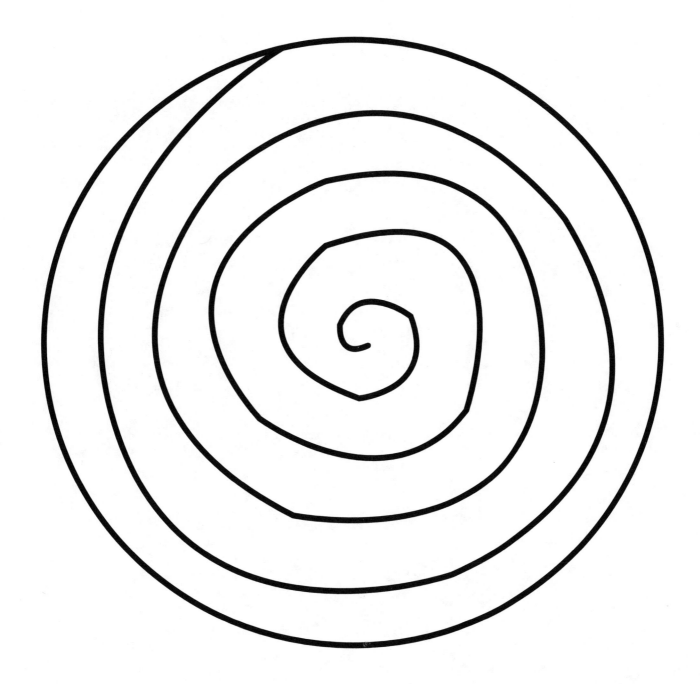

Leaf Patterns

Follow-up Letter

Dear Friend,

Thank you for attending our Fall Festival. It was a pleasure to meet you and we hope that you and your child had a wonderful evening. We have enclosed an evaluation form for you to complete and return to the church if you have any comments you would like to provide to us. We would love to hear from you.

[church name] invites you to attend Sunday morning worship with us. Worship services are held every [day] at [times]. Our children, youth and adults have Sunday school at [times]. We also have [list any other services or related programs, such as children's church or Bible clubs].

Enclosed you will find additional information about our upcoming events such as our Christmas Musical and a special program for children called Christmas Bible School. Please don't hesitate to contact the church office if you would like further information on any of our programs. We look forward to seeing you again.

In Christ's Service,

_____

Name of Director

Beatitudes Beehives

Belly of a Whale

Daniel and the Lions' Den

David and Goliath

Fruits of the Spirit

Fruit of the Spirit

Love	Joy	Peace
Kindness	Goodness	Faithfulness
Self-Control	Hate	Anger
Selfishness	Envy	Meanness
Patience	Gentleness	Jealousy
Love	Joy	Peace
Kindness	Goodness	Faithfulness
Self-Control	Hate	Anger
Selfishness	Envy	Meanness
Patience	Gentleness	Jealousy
Love	Joy	Peace
Kindness	Goodness	Faithfulness
Self-Control	Hate	Anger
Selfishness	Envy	Meanness
Patience	Gentleness	Jealousy
Love	Joy	Peace
Kindness	Goodness	Faithfulness
Self-Control	Hate	Anger
Selfishness	Envy	Meanness
Patience	Gentleness	Jealousy

Good Samaritan

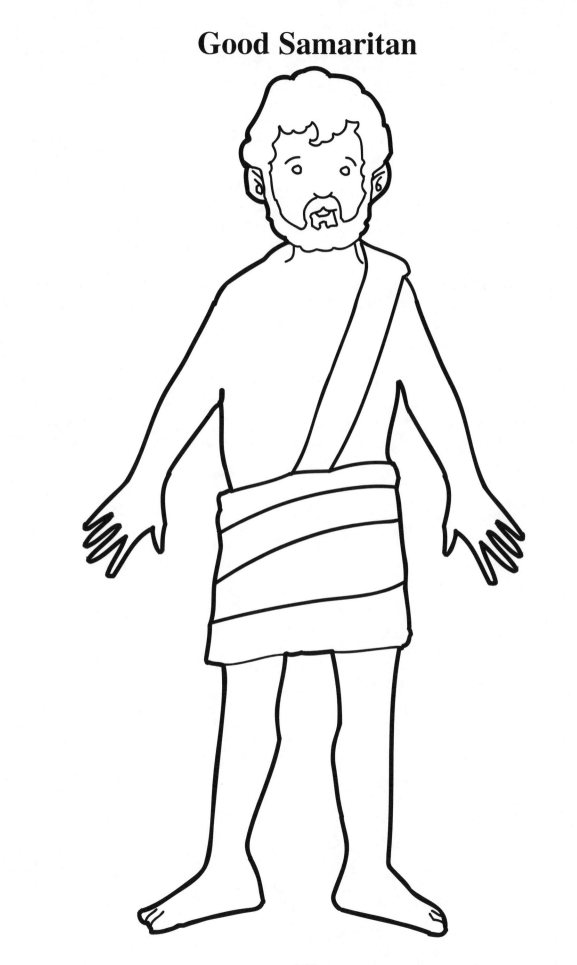

Lost Sheep

Puzzle Piece Search

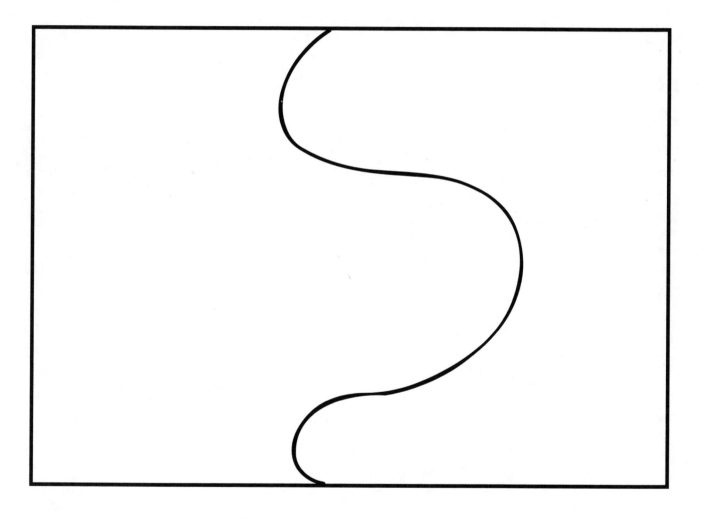

Ten Plagues

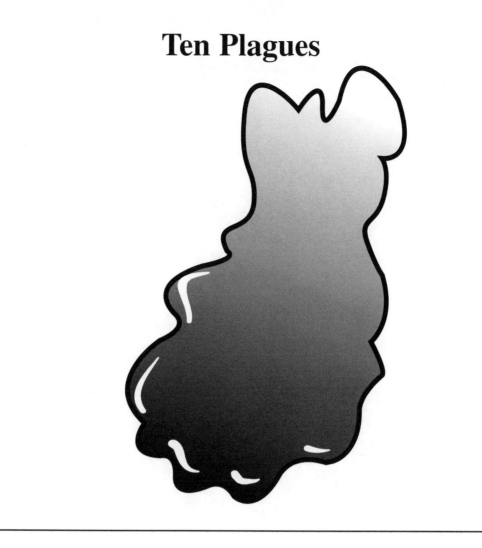

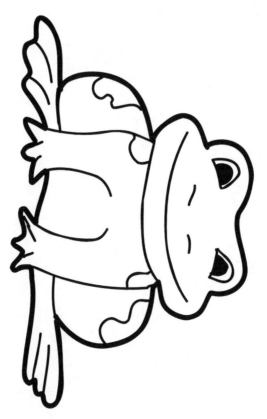

Ten Plagues

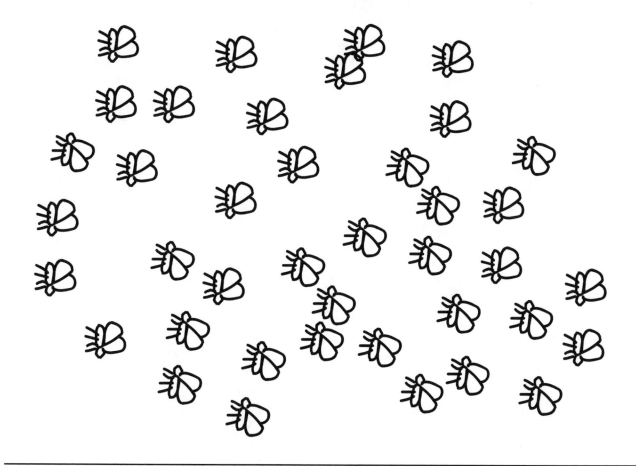

Ten Plagues

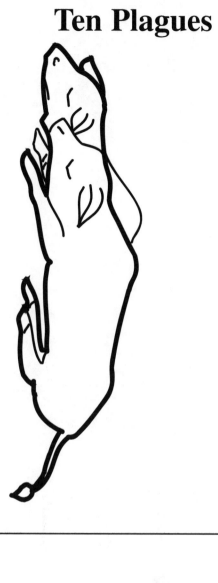

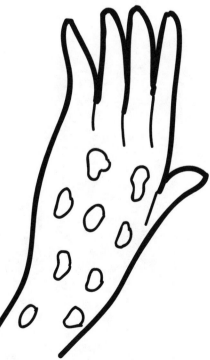

Ten Plagues

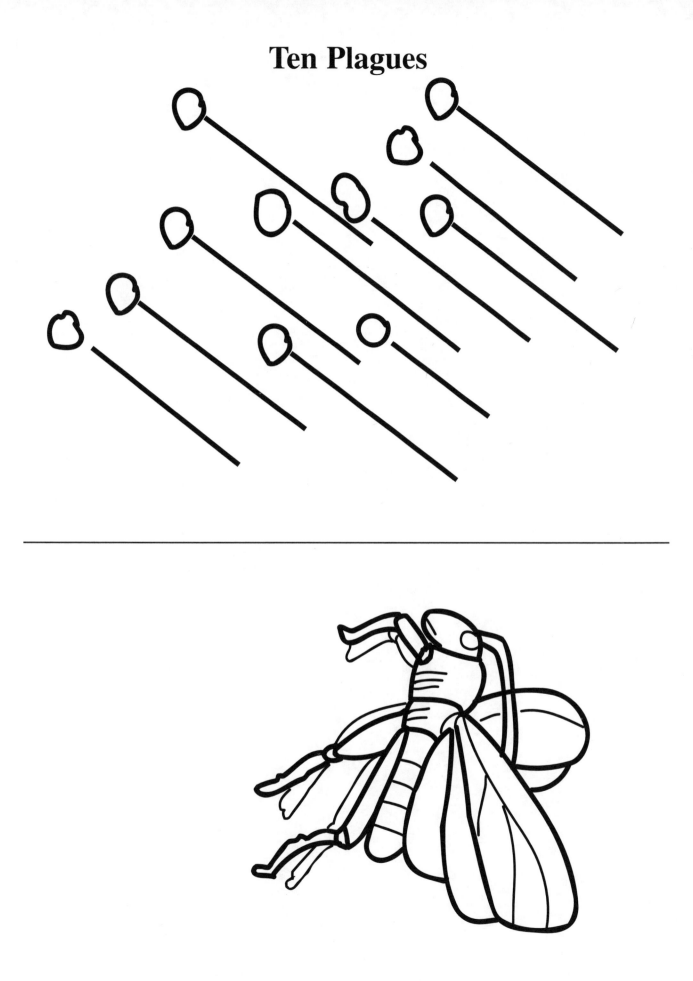

Ten Plagues

Water from the Rock

Wheel of Knowledge

Suggested Questions

Easy

Is the Bible true? (yes)

Whose birthday do we celebrate on Christmas? (Jesus)

What did Noah take on the ark? (animals, food, family)

Who made the world? (God)

How did Jesus die? (On a cross)

What can your parent's read to you that will tell you about Jesus? (Bible)

Hard

What was the name of the giant David killed? (Goliath)

Why was Daniel thrown in the Lion's den? (He would not stop praying to God)

Who led the march around the walls of Jericho? (Joshua)

Name one of the fruits of the Spirit. (love, joy, peace, patience, kindness, goodness, faithfulness, gentleness and self-control)

183

Ark and Animals

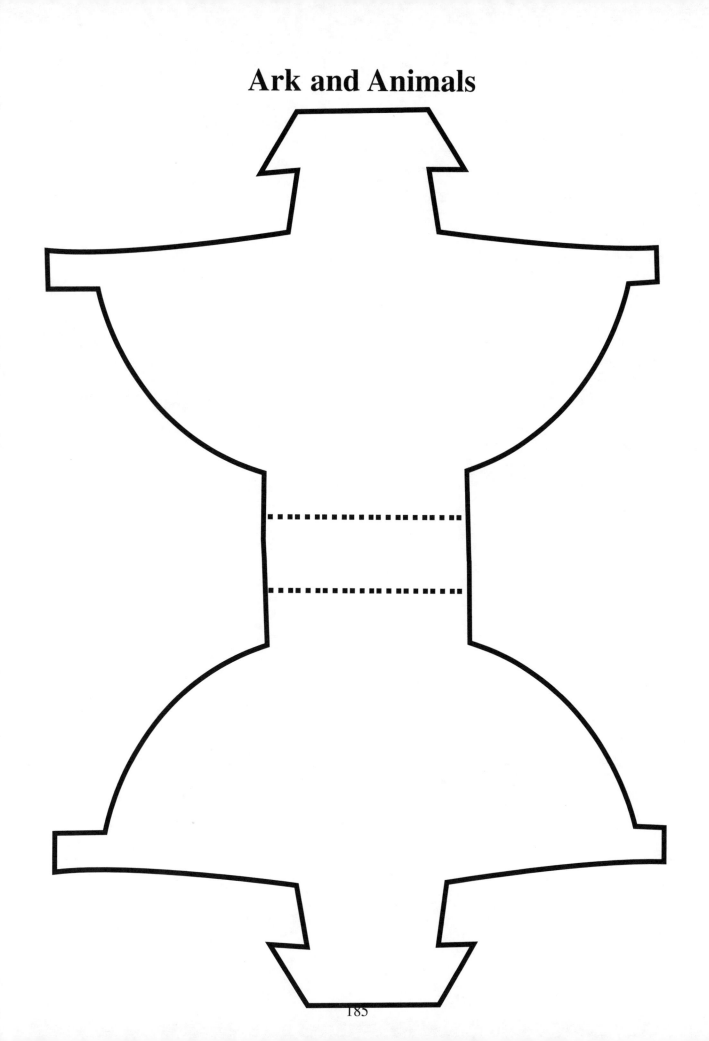

Ark and Animals

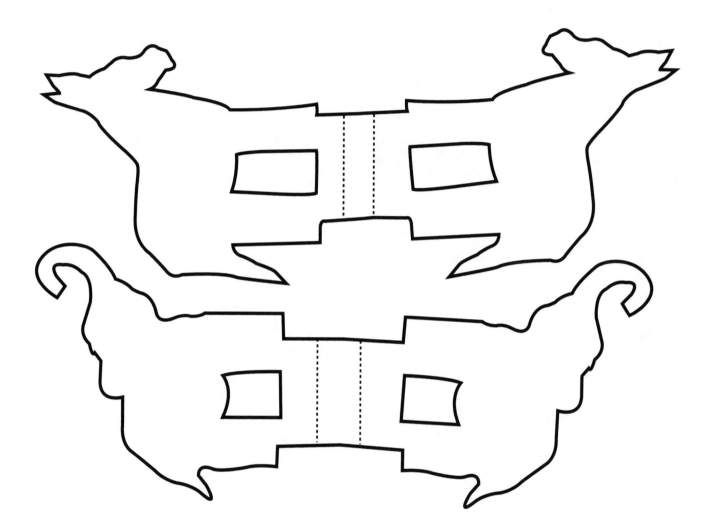

Ark and Animals

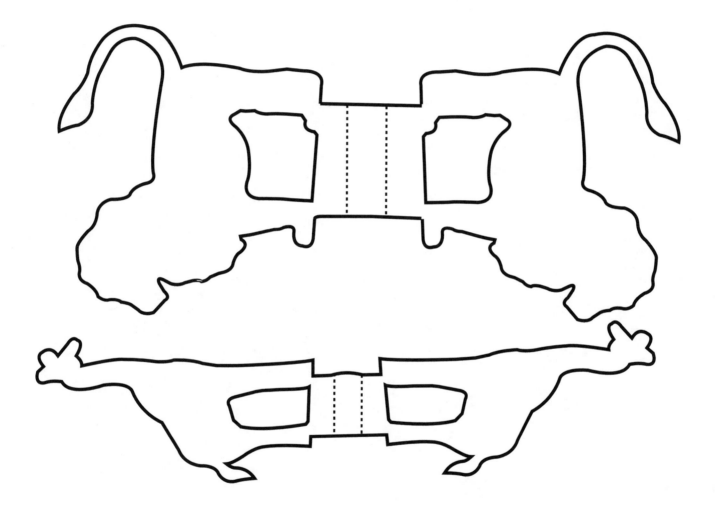

Ark and Animals

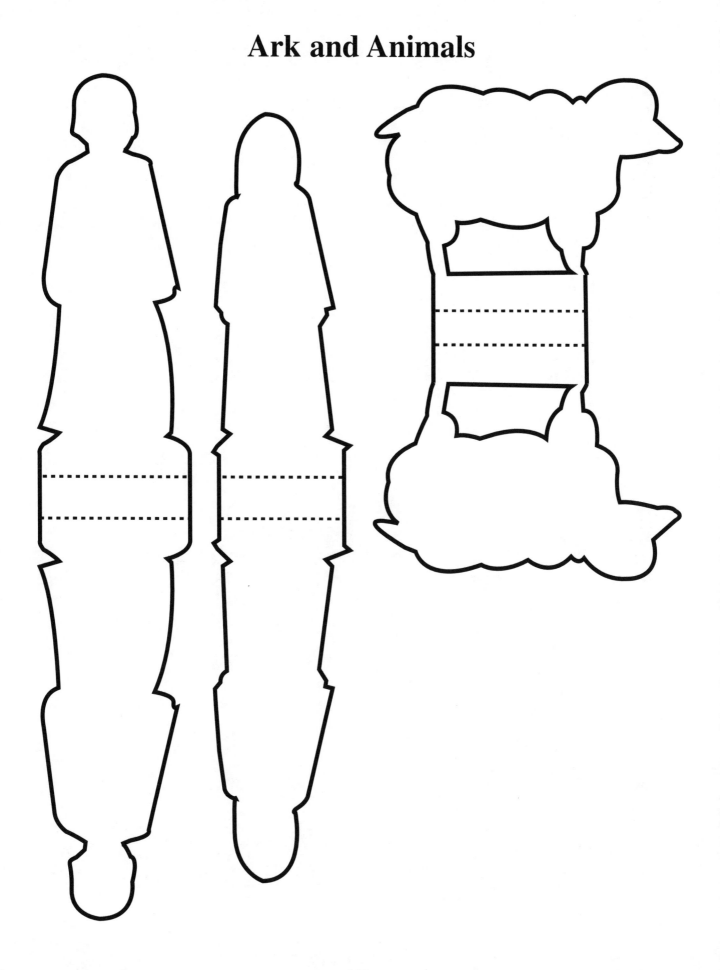

Butterfly Plant Stick

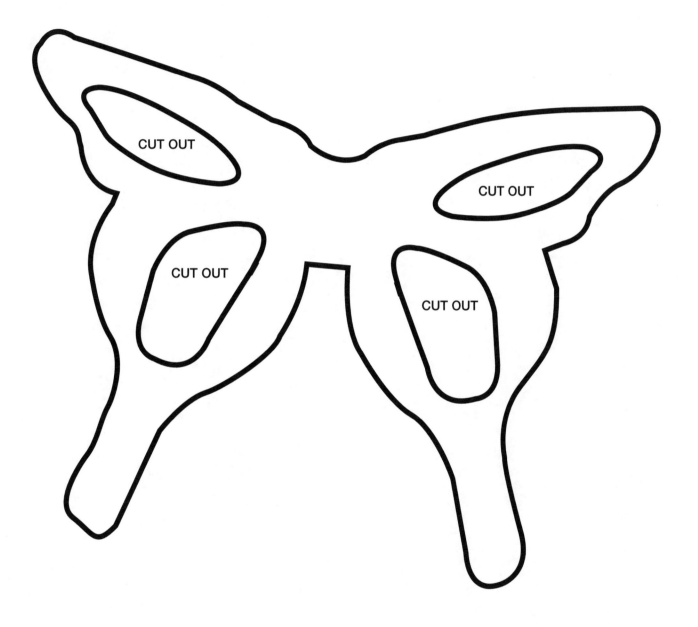

Butterfly Plant Stick

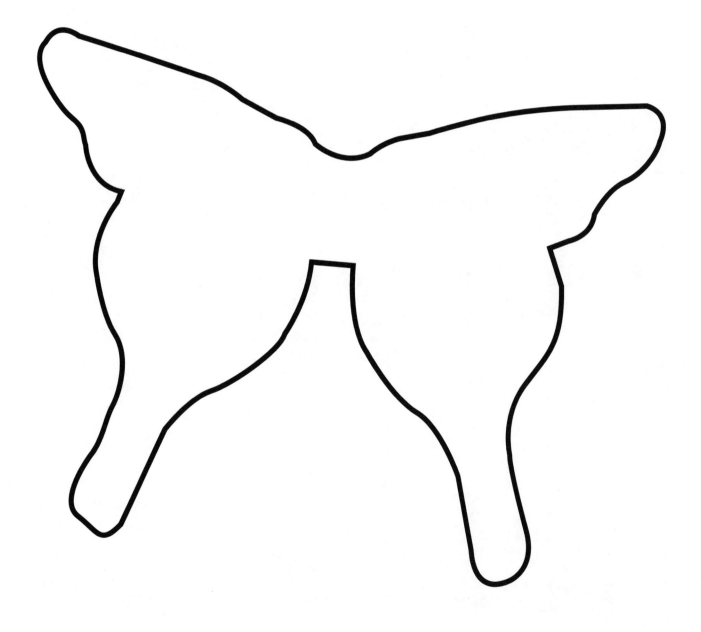

Buzzin' Bees

Good Shepherd Picture Frame

 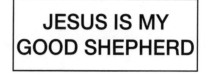

JESUS IS MY
GOOD SHEPHERD

Jonah Pop-up

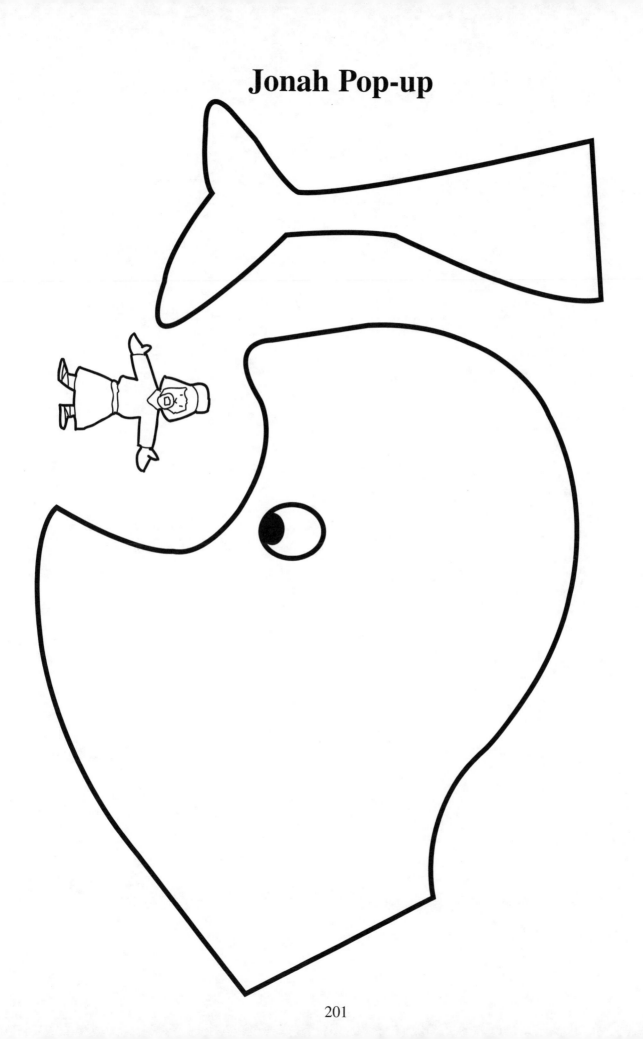

Leaf Mobile

Pom-pom Lion Pencil Topper

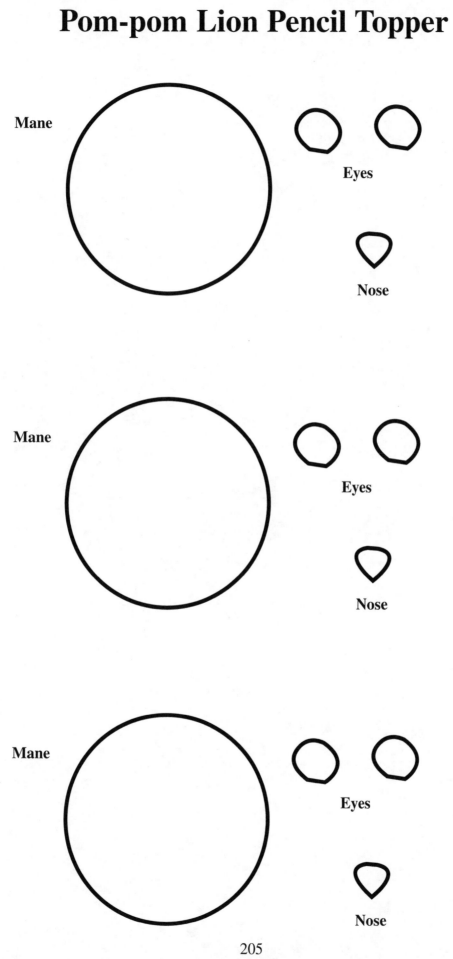

Mane

Eyes

Nose

Mane

Eyes

Nose

Mane

Eyes

Nose

Pumpkin Pin

Stuffed Fish

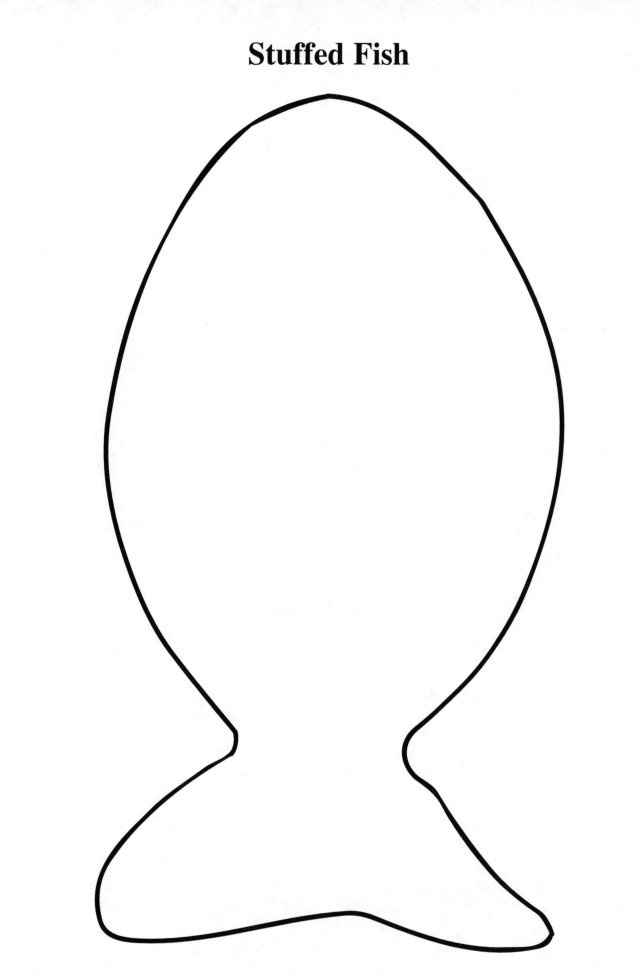

City of Jericho Dot-to-Dot

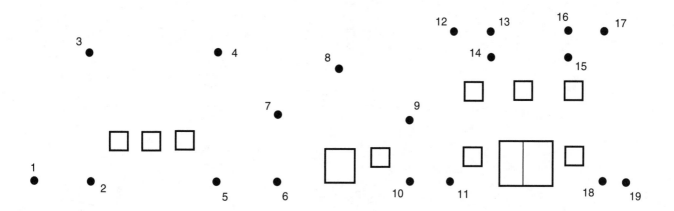

When you hear them sound a long blast on the trumpets, have all the people give a loud shout; then the wall of the city will collapse and the people will go up, every man straight in.
Joshua 6:5

Coded Message

A E L O S U W D H M R T V Y

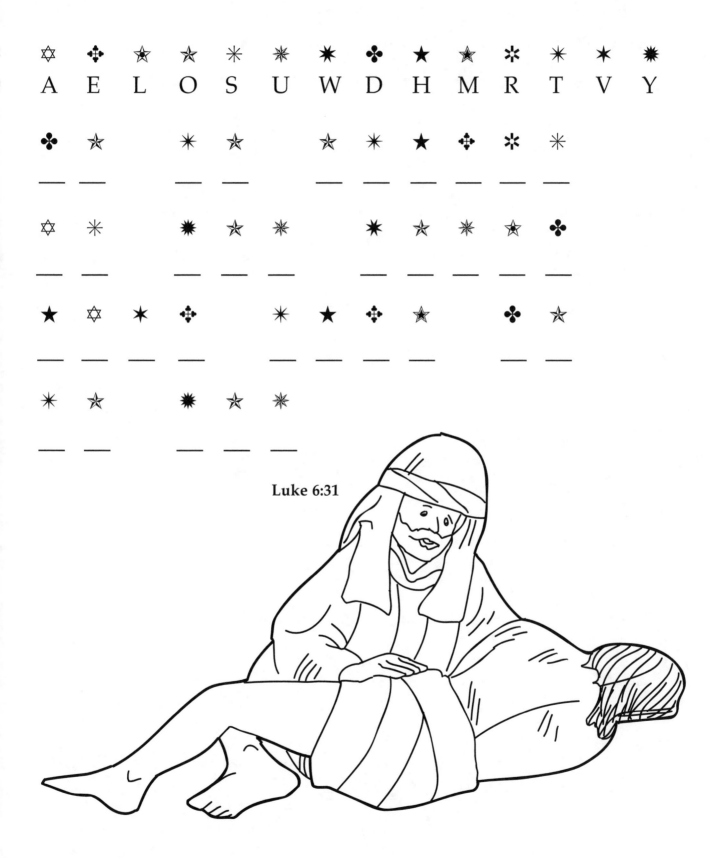

Luke 6:31

David and Goliath

A champion named Goliath, who was from Gath,
came out of the Philistine camp. He was over nine feet tall.
1 Samuel 17:4

Find the Sheep's Twin

I am the good shepherd; I know my sheep and my sheep know me.
John 10:14

217

Fruit of the Spirit Word Search

```
B  D  I  G  P  A  R  D  K  O  A  L  L  N  A
L  O  V  E  C  P  K  J  M  I  G  R  X  P  B
S  B  O  K  K  T  G  O  O  D  N  E  S  S  W
P  E  C  R  Y  I  E  S  T  O  Q  W  A  Z  I
A  B  L  C  F  B  N  U  H  A  C  Y  P  E  C
T  C  O  F  R  Y  T  D  A  N  F  L  K  N  D
I  P  E  R  C  K  L  F  N  E  I  S  N  R  P
E  A  K  S  H  O  E  B  U  E  C  K  I  U  N
N  T  I  T  U  L  N  M  T  S  S  U  P  T  E
C  O  P  E  A  C  E  T  R  E  P  S  A  D  G
E  E  R  L  K  I  S  E  R  B  U  S  M  R  I
Y  O  U  S  P  P  S  W  J  O  Y  R  O  T  K
B  I  P  F  A  I  T  H  F  U  L  N  E  S  S
```

Word List

KINDNESS   GOODNESS
LOVE   FAITHFULNESS
JOY   GENTLENESS
PEACE   SELF-CONTROL
PATIENCE

*But the fruit of the Spirit is love, joy, peace, patience, kindness, goodness,
faithfulness, gentleness and self-control.*
Galatians 5:22-23

How Do They Grow?

How Many Bees?

Blessed are... the poor in spirit

Blessed are... those who mourn

Blessed are... the meek

Blessed are... those who hunger and thirst for righteousness

Blessed are... the merciful

Blessed are... the pure in heart

Blessed are... the peacemakers

Blessed are... those who are persecuted because of righteousness

Mark Out

Mark out the first two letters and circle the third. Continue with this pattern throughout the puzzle. After circling every third letter, copy the circled letters to the blanks below.

OPIuyn wetqrhtye ujsikaolmpme nhwbgavfy, cdlxsezat awyseodruftr gylhuijigkohlpt pmsonhibiuvnyce rebseetpftyouirpke rtmeredsn, wetryhrtafbt mkthjhioetgy zemxracty bysnuemie okyuhoyfufer rtgyuokhogdd sadwreyieopdnbs mvancnczd cspvdrbrantimysmue kkypuootuger GHFeragbtumhomeyvr triewn yghuhetfaesvqcetbn.

—— ——— ————— ——————— ————, ———

———— ——— ———— —————— ———

———————— ———— , ———— —————

——— ———— ———— ————— ————

————— ———— ————— ————— ————

—————— —— —————————.

Matthew 5:16

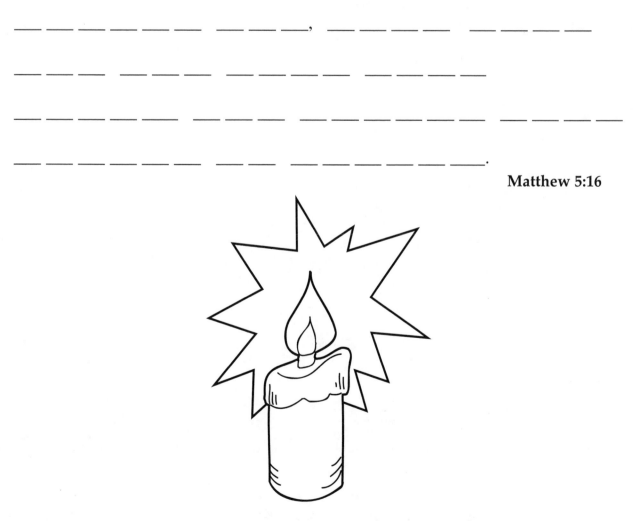

225

Ten Plagues Crossword

ACROSS
1. What you see when you bleed
4. Ruler of Egypt
5. Balls of ice
9. Oldest child
10. Small biting bugs
11. Flying bugs

DOWN
2. Without light
3. Painful swelling on the skin
6. Moses' brother
7. Animals — cows, goats, sheep
8. Grasshoppers
11. Toads

Animal Ears

ELEPHANT

KOALA

LION

231

Animal Ears

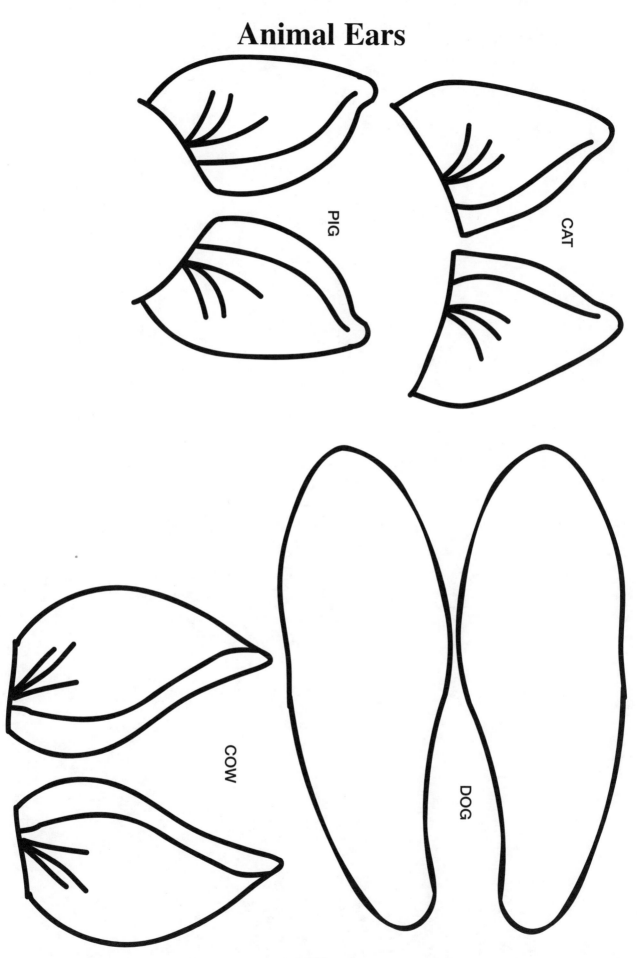

PIG

CAT

COW

DOG

233

Bread of Life

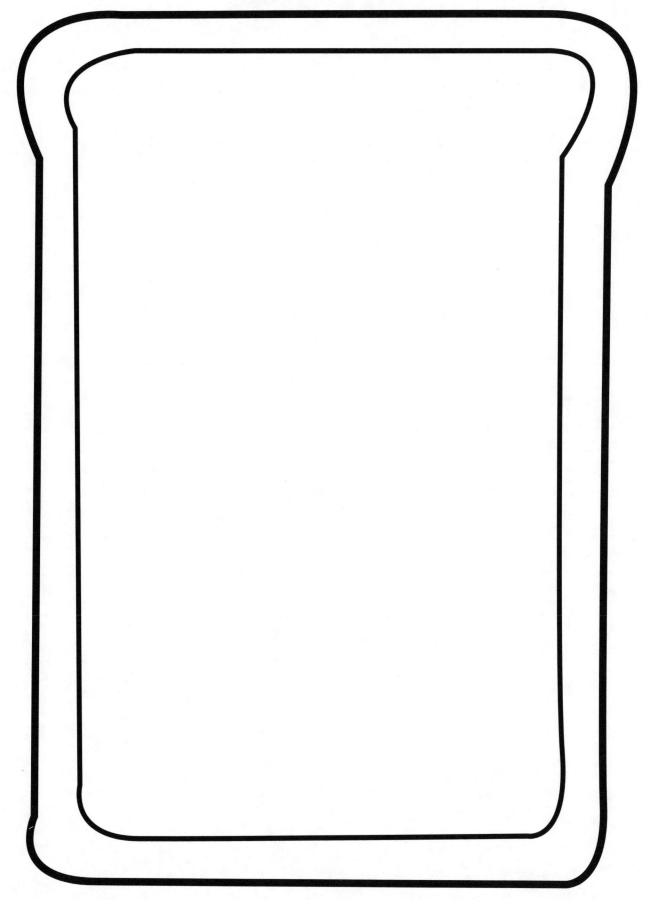

Candle

Roman Soldier Breastplate

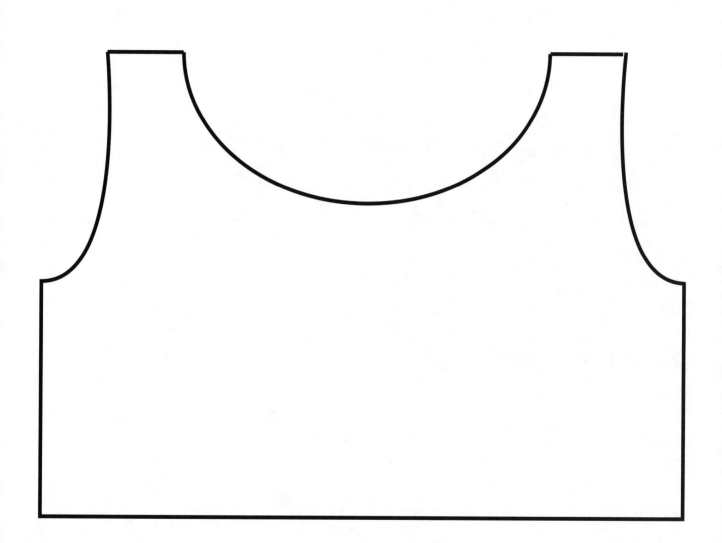

Roman Soldier Ear Piece

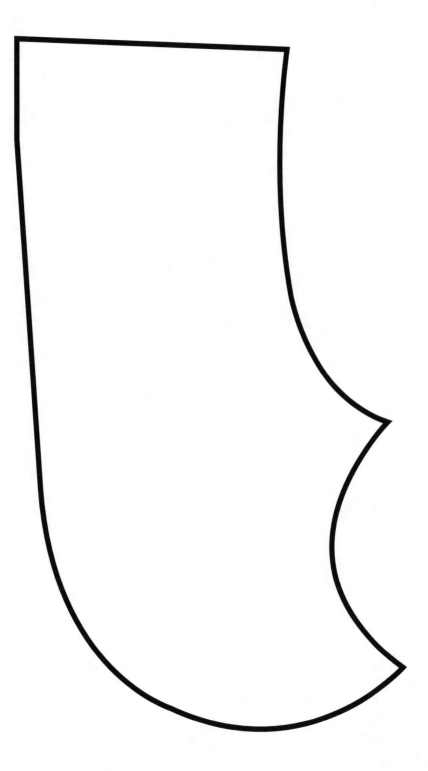

Roman Soldier Helmet

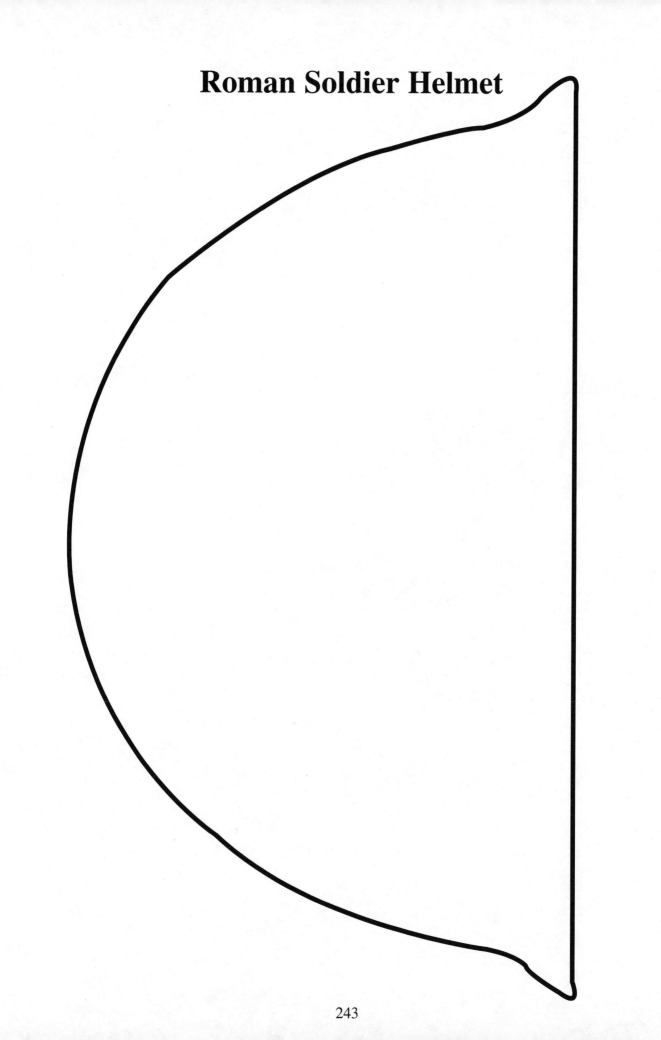

Roman Soldier Skirting

Roman Soldier Triangle

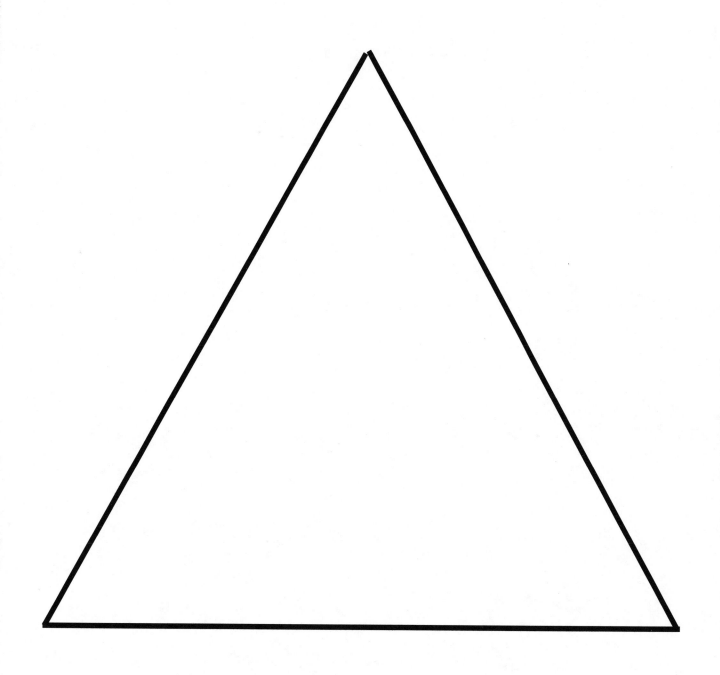